Leadership and Teambuilding: T.
Building a New World

The Presenter's Manual

Manual IV

Books by Victor Vernon Woolf, Ph.D.

Holodynamics: How To Develop and Manage Your Personal Power
The original text

The Dance of Life
Transform your world NOW! Create wellness, resolve conflicts and learn to harmonize your "Being" with Nature.

The Holodynamic State of Being: Manual I
Advocates a course in life that unfolds one's fullest potential for the individual and for the planet.

Presence in a Conscious Universe: Manual II
Detailed training in achieving the state of being present, aligning with one's Full Potential Self, bonding with others, transforming holodynes and unfolding of potential.

Field Shifting: The Holodynamics of Integration: Manual III
Training exercises for integration of field of information from the past, present and future through the relive/prelive processes.

Leadership and Teambuilding: The Holodynamics of Building a New World: Manual IV
The use of a Holodynamic approach within systems as in business and education.

Principle-Driven Transformation: The Holodynamics of The Dance of Life: Manual V
The principles, processes and stories that form the basis for teaching Holodynamics.

The Therapy Manifesto: 95 Treatises on Holodynamic Therapy
An outline of 95 findings from current sciences that apply to the theory and practice of therapy.

The Wellness Manifesto: 95 Treatises on Holodynamic Health
A declaration of findings from current sciences that apply to the health industry.

Elves: The Adventures of Nicholas: The Grid of Agony and The Field of Love
A science fiction story about time-traveling elves who live according to the principles and processes of Holodynamic consciousness and become involved in an intergalactic battle that sweeps a small boy, Nicholas Claus, into shifting the grid of agony into a field of love. How Christmas began.

Intimacy: Develop your Being of Togetherness: How to Create an Open, Dynamic, Effective, Intimate, Living Relationship with Someone You Love

Related Writings

Tracking: The Exploration of the Inner Space by Kirk Rector
The Ten Processes of Holodynamics by Kirk Rector
The above writings can be purchased at www.holodynamics.com/store.asp

LEADERSHIP AND TEAMBUILDING: THE HOLODYNAMICS OF BUILDING A NEW WORLD

THE PRESENTER'S MANUAL
Manual IV

AN INTRODUCTORY COURSE IN
TEACHING HOLODYNAMICS

By
Victor Vernon Woolf, Ph.D.

THE PROCESSES, CONCEPTS, AND PRINCIPLES
BY WHICH A FACILITATOR IN HOLODYNAMICS
BECOMES CERTIFIED
AS A PRESENTER

Leadership and Teambuilding: The Holodynamics of Building a New World

The Presenter's Manual

Original Illustrations by the author
Cover by Charles Montague
Design by Debbie Drecksel
Others by permission as noted

Library of Congress Cataloging-in-Publication Data

Woolf, Victor Vernon
Leadership and Teambuilding: The Holodynamics of Building a New World
The Presenter's Manual
Manual IV

ISBN 0-9746431-4-9
1. Consciousness. 2. Science. 3. Health.
4. Cosmology. 5. Self-Organizing Information Systems.
6. Quantum Theory. 7. Self Help. 8. Title.

PRINTED IN THE UNITED STATES OF AMERICA

Publisher: The International Academy of Holodynamics
1155 West 4th Street, Suite 214, Reno, NV 89503

Additional copies of this text may be obtained directly through www.holodynamics.com or from your local distributor.

TABLE OF CONTENTS

Leadership and Teambuilding: The Holodynamics of Building a New World

THE PRESENTER'S MANUAL

INTRODUCTION

It is obvious to everyone that humanity is undergoing considerable changes. These changes are not just the result of the flood of new inventions and helpful technologies that have become available in the last few decades. Nor are these changes limited to the melting of old organizational structures, governments and corporate cultures. What is happening is that a major revolution is occurring in human consciousness. We are literally birthing a new world. This text is about that birthing process. It serves as the text for the fourth *Circle of Success* in the series sponsored by the International Academy of Holodynamics.

The first *Circle of Success* focused on the new information from science that reveals reality as a multidimensional, interconnected, holographic, conscious matrix made of information in motion. Evidence shows that solutions to even our most complex problems are within enfolded dimensions of reality. These enfolded dimensions include the holographic dimension, the hyperspacial dimension and the multiple dimensions of consciousness. We live in a conscious, interconnected, dynamic universe.

The second *Circle* outlined the various schools of thought regarding human consciousness and explored how the various mechanisms of consciousness function. The role of the microtubules of the body were explored where holographic images (holodynes) proved to be quantum, self-organizing and self-perpetuating units of cause. We discussed how holodynes control all human behavior and grow according to an implicate order. We discussed how holodynes can be transformed and we outlined the role of the Consultant in the transformation process.

The third *Circle* dealt with collective consciousness. We discussed how entire information fields can be shifted and transformed through processes such as the "relive" and "prelive" processes. Everything is *in relationship,* and our focus was on the transformation of the most intimate of relationships between couples. A Facilitator does Field shifting and we defined in some detail how this is accomplished.

This fourth *Circle of Success* addresses leadership and team building. This manual presents a model for conducting business that moves beyond the linear self-interest and into a new, multidimensional approach to business, which produces a more sustainable future for everyone.

We are in the middle of the birth of a new world. Part of this birthing process is the amazing flood of new information and the resulting advances of new technologies that have occurred over the last few decades. Another part of this new world is the role being played by what is termed "the corporate mentality" that is dominated by linear thinking and consumed with its own self-interest. The result is that the "collective consciousness of business" has taken these new technologies and uses them to expand their power into networks of international dominance. The price of this limited collective mentality is that life is not sustainable under this type of leadership. Even more alarming is the fact that collective self-interest is threatening the balance of the biosphere. Humans have become the most devastating influence that life on the planet has experienced in over 65 million years. We could die in the birthing process.

What has yet to emerge in this birthing process is a state of consciousness that will result in a more sustainable future. We know how to overcome pollution, cure most diseases, educate every child, overcome poverty and can sculpt our societies so that we can live beyond war. The knowledge is available on how to create a sustainable future but what we have yet to learn is how to develop the fullest potential of our consciousness so we can implement what we know. This fourth Circle of Success is about mastering the type of consciousness that will produce more expanded awareness of our collective consciousness, build relationships that are more effective, develop businesses that are more conscientious and create a future we can all live with.

Since information organizes from the micro to the macro, we will begin with potentializing the course of your personal life and teaming up to meet your own prime conditions. Our focus will then expand to business in general; and how to create synergistic systems with effective strategic planning according to the natural implicate order of business. We explore how to transform our collective mentality about business and leadership. This Circle will also demonstrate how to teach this information to others. We outline two courses in detail: one for the public and the other for advanced corporate development.

Five books precede this text:

1. *Holodynamics; How to Develop and Manage your Personal Power*
2. *The Dance of Life; Transform your world NOW!*
3. *Manual I: The Holodynamic State of Being;*
4. *Manual II: Presence in a Conscious Universe;* and
5. *Manual III: Field Shifting: The Holodynamics of Integration.*

These texts (see References) are available through the Academy as well as from your local bookstores. In preparation for this course, which is the fourth Circle of Success, we recommend that you read these five texts and learn the skills associated with each Circle. Once exposed to this information, you must make a commitment to *take the course of your Full Potential Self* because, in this *Circle,* you will be asked to become *present* in the business arena and to teach others to do the same.

The world is in the process of rebirthing itself. New information is flooding in upon us. A smorgasbord of opportunity is spread before us. We get to choose our future. This is a good time to be present.

CHAPTER ONE

POTENTIALIZING THE COURSE OF YOUR LIFE

BIRTHING A NEW WORLD DOES NOT MEAN WE NEED A NEW WORLD. I LIKE THE ONE WE HAVE. In fact, I think this world is perfect in every way. Of course, I look at "problems"as being "caused by their solutions," so problems are invitations to me - invitations to find the solutions – and, for me, finding solutions to complex problems is one of the more exciting things to do on this planet.

As I read the information from the new sciences, I find all kinds of indications that each of the difficulties we face was actually planned *by us* for our benefit. How else could we ever be challenged to create the solutions? When you step back and look at the whole dynamic of life, it is magnificent. Everything is information in motion. Every subatomic particle, all matter and life - everything - is made of a dynamic information matrix.

One of the most exciting things about this world is constant change and, in this era, the change has accelerated. It is global. It is a rebirth. The entire life grid of information is shifting and every living thing on the planet is participating. You and I were born to steward part of this process. I sit and write and, in these writings, I participate in the birthing of the new world. We organize classes, build education and health systems, create new communication networks among wonderful people, build teams with a purpose in mind, overcome diseases, transform pollution into valuable products, develop new forms of pollutant-free transportation, create new energy sources and a more sustainable future and all of it is part of the rebirthing process.

Exercise 1: Birthing a new world.

Imagine yourself in a Place of Peace. Leave your body there, in your Place of Peace, and travel above the world. As you look down upon the world, sense the people in all their varieties, living and moving about the planet.

Can you sense their thoughts and feelings, hopes and dreams? Can you experience the anguish and terror, anger and frustration, as well as their love and devotion, faith and hope?

Can you imagine a panoramic view of the history of humanity? Can you sense the rise and fall of nations and races, and see how everything has led to this moment in time?

Now imagine yourself able to sense other life forms on the planet: the plants and animals, insects and microbes, and life in all its varieties. Can you sense various species? Can you allow yourself to imagine the emergence of each species, its adaptation to its environment, and even the reflection of its extinction? Can you allow yourself to appreciate the biosphere in which we live and have our being?

Imagine a planet in which the harmony and balance of life is realized. What would be happening on such a planet? How would it be different from the one on which we now reside?

If this planet were to "birth" itself into a new planet, what would you like to change? What could it be like? Make notes in your journal. Then discuss your impressions with a partner and with a team. How are your impressions similar? In what ways, if any, do they differ?

In each of the manuals prior to this one, I have emphasized the advantages to "taking the course" of your Full Potential Self. In the first manual, the emphasis was on accessing your Full Potential Self as part of your daily consciousness and life planning. In the second manual, the focus was more on potentializing your holodynes and using their power to align with your Full Potential Self. With the primary relationships of your internal world in order, the third manual focused upon relationships - both among your internal holodynes and with your external partners. The key point was how to shift field dynamics of these relationships.

We now will explore how to potentialize this world of relationships. Life is about relationships. Relationships control the field dynamics of reality. Once you have learned about holodynes, field dynamics, and potentialization, it becomes possible to address *how to potentialize the course of your life.*

Exercise 2: Review of the teachings of the Dance of Life and the first three manuals:

Organize into a discussion group of about five people. Make sure that at least one member of the group has studied the text and the first three manuals. Identify those members of the group who have taken any of the first three Holodynamic courses.

Review together the processes of establishing a Place of Peace, connecting with your Full Potential Self, how to use tracking, reliving and preliving and the other processes of Holodynamics. Make sure everyone in your group has at least a basic understanding of these processes. (Do NOT get caught up in performing the processes at this time).

After your review and discussion, imagine yourself once again traveling through space high above the planet. Imagine, this time, that you are viewing the world in a time before you were born.

Imagine your task was to choose a time a place in which you were to be born. What era of time would you choose? Based on what would you make that choice?

Imagine your task was to choose a family into which you are going to be born. What race would you choose? What parents would you choose? What siblings would you choose?

You can ask a lot of questions about this: How much money would you want your fam-

ily to have? What level of education would your parents have? What friends would you choose? What career(s) would you want? How much money would you want to make? Would you want to inherit vast wealth or would you want to make it? And so on.

Discuss your journey with your team. What conclusions do you reach? Write them down.

One of the encouraging things about life is that we are still *at choice point*. Living with your holodynes and with others in this space-time continuum can be far more interesting than most people realize. You can literally rebirth your entire life. In doing so, you become a more intimate part of the rebirthing of the planet. The first step in potentializing your life is to *establish your own prime conditions through potentializing each relationship.*

Establishing your Prime Condition

Establishing your Prime Condition means opening the field of your potential so that you can unfold that potential you choose. In a sense, it is like having all your needs fulfilled at every level of development for life. This allows you to be at "choice point." You can choose what you will do in life.

On the physical level, this means having the money you want to spend, the home of your dreams, the car and other transportation needs you may desire, as well as having the job you want, your business expenses taken care of, the food you want, and all other physical needs fulfilled. When your physical prime conditions are met, you are free from the slavery of survival mentalities and are more able to spend your time, effort and resources in whatever creative endeavors YOU choose.

At the personal level, it means having your personal, emotional, intellectual and developmental needs met. It means overcoming all those hidden "reasons" for not being happy, for downdrafting and playing self-destructive games. It means being *present* at your fullest potential as the person your really are capable of being. This includes having good friends, a supportive community and a world we can be proud of as participants. If this sounds euphoric, rest assured that it is not and idle fantasy. Setting your prime conditions is a reality you can create for yourself. You can also have your relationship needs, the degree of intimacy you desire, the quality of life in society and the love you want. This is the natural state of humans.

It means you are able to respond to principle-driven scenarios, guide your life with faith and love, and overcome any barriers to your own integrity. You can understand life, and you can be aligned with its fullest potential. You can extend yourself out as far as you like, into the world. You can create a mission, join with others, fulfill your dreams, and establish the kind of world you want now and for the generations to come.

This Manual is about how to do exactly that - establish Prime Conditions - for life. Establishing your Prime Condition is to create the foundation; have the money, friends and systems you need to exercise your prime right to be free. Free to self-improve and create whatever you choose, free to function at your fullest potential and free to hold a field for others to do the same. You are free to share this information with others.

Exercise 3: Identify your Prime Conditions

Using the Mind Model and particularly the Six Stages of Development of Consciousness (refer to Manuals I, II and III), identify what you consider to be your Prime Conditions at each stage of development.

PHYSICAL PRIME CONDITIONS:

These items assume that your business, investment, and entire portfolio are secured. The first item, for example, assumes that the amount of money you would like just to "spend" as "play money" would be extra. Your home, in the second item, should be described and the amount necessary to clear your mortgage, so you have it free and clear, should be outlined. Transportation means your car, boat, plane or other means of transportation. How much money would it take to "set" your prime conditions and have it so you are free to do what you want?

AMOUNT SPENDING MONEY EACH MONTH	$/MONTH
HOME	
TRANSPORTATION	
OTHER: (list)	

Create a collage, from magazines or from your own drawings of your home, car and other physical items that you sense are part of your prime conditions. Include it in this manual.

PERSONAL PRIME CONDITIONS:

List below those conditions you sense must be met in order for you to unfold to the fullest extent, your personal potential.

EDUCATION	
HOBBIES	
INTERESTS	
OTHERS	

RELATIONSHIP PRIME CONDITIONS:

List below what you consider to be the prime conditions you must set in order for you to meet the fullest potential of your Being of Togetherness (BOT) or to have a personal, intimate, empowered relationship with a significant other.

LEVEL OF COMMITMENT	
OPENNESS	
HONESTY	
SUPPORT	
HOLDING A FIELD	
OTHERS	

SYSTEMS PRIME CONDITIONS:

Consider the systems to which you are currently connected or to which you would like to become connected. What systems do you consider desirable in meeting your prime conditions?

JOB	
COMMUNITY	
SPIRITUAL SUPPORT	
THE NATURAL WORLD	
OTHERS	

PRINCIPLE PRIME CONDITIONS:

What principles do you sense you would like to achieve in order to be present and integritous in your life?

LOVE	
RESPONSIBILITY	
CLARITY	
INTEGRITY	
OTHERS	

UNIVERSALITY:

Each of us has the possibility of extending our influence into the universe. As you align with the fullest potential of the universe, what do you sense might be necessary in order for you to align with the potential of life and help to manifest its fullest potential.

ONENESS	
UNDERSTANDING	
STATE OF BEING MORE ALIVE TO LIFE	
OTHERS	

As you complete the above exercise, go back over the list you have made. Using the Mind Model, consider the specific actions you can take in order to prepare a plan to set your prime conditions. Can you find a way to measure your results? (This is a particle approach). How will you feel once your prime conditions are set? (This is a wave approach). Finally, go to your Place of Peace and ask your Full Potential Self if each item is in alignment with the course your Full Potential Self wants you to take in life (the presence approach). Note any changes, suggested by your Full Potential Self.

As we have discussed in prior manuals, all information is self-organizing into holodynes that come from inheritance (through the microtubules of the sperm and the egg), are modeled for us by our family and culture, come from parallel worlds and can be created by our own experiences. This reservoir of holodynes forms into networks of interaction that have their own boundaries (event horizons), forming a matrix or field of information that holds consciousness in patterns. This is what gives us coherence.

When we make a conscious choice, our focus feeds into this field and activates the holodynes that control our thoughts, feelings and behavior. We are part of an active, holographic information system that is multidimensional and inseparably connected to hyperspace. Everything we can see, taste, touch, hear or smell is made of spinners of information that are holographic and in constant motion. Holodynes control most of our lives. The good news is that we can create our own holodynes.

Exercise 4: Create a holodyne wherein your Prime Conditions are set.

Imagine your state of being in which your prime conditions are already met. What would it look like? How would it feel? Would you be able to function more fully as your Full Potential Self?

What color would such a state of being reflect? What shape would it take? Can you draw the form of this new state of being? Draw it below:

The FORM of the holodyne in which my prime conditions are set is as follows:

Invite this new holodyne to sit with you at your Round Table in your Place of Peace. Ask it if it willing to communicate with you on a daily, moment-by-moment basis. Will it help you to establish the setting of all your prime conditions and the manifestation of everything you want in life?

Will it agree to be guided by the same principles you want to see established in setting of your own prime conditions? Will it align with your fullest potential? If it agrees, welcome it to your Round Table and agree to start and end each day with a discussion about what is needed and a progress report on setting of your prime conditions. If it has any messages for you at this time, write them in your journal.

Blocks to the Setting of your Prime Conditions

If you are caught in an event horizon (a "closed bubble" of information), you are trapped. You can only access the information *within* the event horizon. It is self-organizing. It controls your perception, giving you limited view, curtailing your sensitivity and your ability to respond to the dynamics of life. You get comfortable with it. You fall into the habit of being "on cruise control." When this happens, you must take a superposition so that you can think bigger that the problem. The most effective way to do this is to create a Place of Peace and use it to access the hyperspacial dimension so you can consciously connect with your Full Potential Self. Then you have access to an expanded reality.

Event horizons are not isolated to your internal state of mind, nor are they limited to their own internal field dynamics. Event horizons are all connected within the potential field. In previous manuals, I have discussed in some detail how such connections take place in the quantum field and they find their manifestation within our microtubules. The microtubules within the cells of our bodies (and all living things) are one of the central mechanisms of consciousness. Microtubules contain our holodynes.

Holodynes are formed as multidimensional graphics. The media for these graphics is the pure water molecules within the microtubules. Holodynes are held in place and protected from environmental contamination by the dimer molecules that make up the wall of the microtubule. At the same time, holodynes can manipulate the valence of the dimers (they become positive in valence when they open, negative in valence when they close, and neutral in valence when they are in between). In this way, the dimers are involved in establishing memory as sets of information fields that are held in place by valence fields much like in a computer chip, except that the body uses water as its media and not silicon.

In addition, holodynes have certain "channels" opened for input and output of information. They use a Gaborian-type transform and can send and receive messages throughout our entire bodies because they "resonate" with certain quantum frequencies (Frohlech Frequencies). Thus they create the quantum coherence of who we are and they even control and correlate all of our senses and how we perceive and experience life.

What this means is that as soon as you consciously decide to set your prime conditions, you will ignite certain holodynes. Some of these holodynes will begin to create your prime conditions and some will resist the necessary changes. Under normal circumstances, your "gatekeeper" holodynes will attempt to block any change.

Gatekeepers keep the system stable, maintain order and don't like shifts in the field dynamics. Over time, they come to think they run the show. You must learn to identify and, through love and appreciation, help these gatekeepers to align with your new state of being. They are, after all, part of your state of being.

Exercise 5: Identify and Transform your Gatekeepers

The tracking process for identifying and transforming those holodynes that are blocking your from setting your prime conditions is outlined in detail in Manual II. If you cannot believe you can set your prime conditions and if you feel like it is not possible or it is unbelievable, or any other number of thoughts or feelings you may be experiencing that tell you it is not possible for you to meet your prime conditions, cluster these feelings and thoughts and the issues they represent. Then ask for assistance from a Consultant to identify and track each of the holodynes involved.

Note: This process can be endless since you can, theoretically, call up any holodynes from any field. So to stay on purpose, learn the process and allow your internal system to self-organize so it does most of the work. Use your Full Potential Self as your guide. Maintain a supportive and cooperative role but do not become lost in the endless tracking possibility. It is essential, however, that you personally study, experience and master the tracking process. In your journal, create space for these subjects:

My gatekeepers are:

Tracking notes:

Overcoming Collective Resistance

Within our microtubules, information from holodynes can enter hyperspacial dimensions and then spread from one person to another. Thus holodynes become *collective*. Collective holodynes are the keys to public opinion, consensus and collective consciousness. They are transmitted from one generation to another, reinforced and carried as family and cultural belief systems and are thus a part of every society. They are also inherited and passed on from one generation to the next and from one world to the next.

Some of these collectively held holodynes become Gatekeepers. This means we can be caught in endless struggle, sacrifice and war games because there are holodynes within the event horizon that are embedded in us, within our information systems. The Gatekeepers want to keep things the way they are. They "play with our minds" so to speak and distract us from setting our prime conditions.

All of us are subject to such games. Our life energy can get "downdrafted" and we can cycle endlessly, caught in their dynamics. Thus ignorance, disease and humankind's inhumanity toward each other and toward nature is now embedded within every person and within every culture. They run our businesses and network our corporations. These holodynes have formed a collective consciousness that now threatens the life of the planet. Some people would rather, it seems, have the planet die than rebirth themselves into their next stage of development.

We are challenged to solve this problem. We *must*, if we want to survive. In reality, we were born to meet this challenge. It is part of the Covenant. But it will never happen unless *you* decide, internally, that you are going to *set your own prime conditions*. This personal, deep decision ignites the Gatekeepers of the entire collective. They understand that for one person to set his or her prime conditions *means the entire field must shift*. Things must change on a larger, collective scale. These Gatekeepers can become a very real problem because their collective is dysfunctional. They are a major part of the reason we are locked into our collective pathologies. They can sabotage even our very best attempts unless they are transformed and brought into alliance with our personal potential.

To solve the problem of collective dysfunction requires teamwork. It requires a new collective consciousness more capable of timely self-correction. Collective holodynes and their event horizons can only be self-corrective by micro systems (teams) that are aligned with their fullest potentials. When a team aligns with full potential, each individual aligns with their own Full Potential Self. Then team members choose specific things they would like to see manifest in the world and they go to work to make it happen. They choose a mission and put their mind, heart and resources into manifesting their objectives.

It is within the *heat* of purposeful potentialization that the blocking holodynes of the collective emerge. In a way, to declare a purposeful mission is taken as a declaration of war on the Gatekeepers of conformity. All those holodynes who "keep the gates" of the "city of stability" become awakened to the "threat" of change. In other words, to change the field is to invite an opposite and equal resistance to the change.

As the team moves toward self-correcting the collective pathologies within the field, those holodynes that hold the field become even more active. Thus, team members who understand how to accept, include and automatically potentialize their holodynes (through tracking, "reliving" and "preliving", for example) are able to move through the resistance and to self-correct the whole collective dynamic.

Those who understand that the world is Holodynamic are able to make the distinctions necessary to move beyond collectively embedded holodynes. The entire team can shift field dynamics beyond individual efforts. They move beyond the keepers of the gates.

When you, as an individual, align with the collective of the team, you challenge the boundaries of the event horizon. The comfort zones of your old community holodynes begin to dissolve into chaos. The mission either expands outward and begins to create new event horizons or it collapses inward and the team begins to fall apart. This happens within entire societies and nations.

In America, for example, the creation and collapse of event horizons takes place continually and on a relatively small scale. It is going on all the time, day by day, in the marketplace and on the stock exchange. Small businesses, for example, that make up the majority of the Gross National Product of the United States are continually starting up and breaking down. Contracts are made, products produced and sold, and companies fold. More than 98 percent of new businesses fail within the first two years in the United States. Only the most creative of efforts sees a business begin and succeed over time.

In Russia, on the other hand, the Gross National Product has been the responsibility of the collective society. The government decides what is done and it is done. Products, such as pencils, for example, are produced in huge government plants built mostly during the Stalin era. A single type of pencil was manufactured in a plant with more than a million employees. It takes another million people to support the population of the pencil plant (food, clothing, shelter, transportation, materials, distribution, etc.) This seemed like a wonderful idea to those who worked within the ideal of Communism.

The trouble began when a particular product became obsolete. The little yellow pencil was being replaced by an automated pencil with replaceable lead. With the demand for the yellow pencil diminishing in the market place, the entire plant was required to shift its focus to new products. It meant that more than two million people's jobs were at risk.

To make the problem worse, the massive machinery became outdated or worn out. Have you ever driven a 50-year-old car? Unless you have it completely restored, it has to be held together by wire and nursed through its motions. The massive plants of the former Soviet Union grew old. There was no money available to have them restored since their products were outdated. They were being nursed every day by employees who had been on the same job their entire lives. When a large plant closes down, potentially millions of people are out of work. When an entire system of such plants begins to falter, the entire country falters.

The difference is clear. A series of small failures is easier to manage than a series of large failures. The American system proved more flexible in an Information Age in which change is rapid and structures must remain flexible.

This rapid influx of information on a global scale has created a new field of consciousness. A new world of information is now available to more and more people on the planet. We now live in a world with new products, new possibilities, new alliances and strategic networks and new freedoms. It is now possible for everyone to have a good education, high quality information, health care and economic independence. It is the birthing of a new world, one in which every person can set his or her prime conditions. For the first time in history, it becomes possible for people to self-initiate a new collective consciousness that *self-corrects* its own pathologies.

It starts with everyone deciding to set their own prime conditions and then going for it with all their heart, mind and strength. This individual action begins the process. It clicks into the collective and sends waves into the field dynamics. Then, in order to be successful over time, it requires small teams of flexible people who understand the Holodynamics of their inner world, who know how to focus, and who have the discipline to commit to a mission and manifest what they want. These are the *potentializer's* of the future, who are capable of potentializing every situation until their mission is accomplished.

As a potentializing participant, you understand that as you move beyond the shell or your own holodynes, you can access your *source*, your Full Potential Self, and view the world in terms of *unfolding potential*. You discover and experience the *dynamic* dimension of reality. Your Full Potential Self begins to have a clearer voice, more influence in your life, and you learn to be an **Advocate** of *taking the course* of your Full Potential Self. The result is you begin to reflect a fuller, richer life in a Holodynamic universe.

Once you realize you are living in a Holodynamic universe, one that is whole and dynamic, you discover you can *access* those *holodynes* that block the unfolding of your potential, learn to transform them, and align fully with your Full Potential Self.

As your own horizons expand, the joy and fullness you feel compels you to became a **Consultant** in order to teach others these vital skills of self-transformation of inner thought forms. As you share with others, even in the sharing, you "get" what you share. You further transform yourself by helping others to transform. To "transform" means to "change the form" of the information that is controlling your experience of reality.

As you become more aware of the field dynamics of sharing, you begin to notice the *spinner effect,* and this is where the science of vortex energies and field dynamics help to wrap words around what you are experiencing. Everything becomes information in motion. Everything becomes *in relationship* and the processes of how we, as individuals, can make a difference, becomes a major focus. Thus the processes of how to *shift the field,* "*relive*" *the past and* "*prelive*" *the future* become powerful tools in the transforming of your information dynamics and thus in the unfolding your personal potential.

You become a **Facilitator** of field shifting. Your natural state of being reaches out. You begin to help others learn to facilitate their own field shifts. You watch as they become empowered in relationship to the ever-changing dynamics in the new emerging consciousness of a world that is in the process of rebirthing or transforming.

In this manual, we take the next natural step. We begin to explore *reality* as *information in motion* and we open to the possibility that *every set of circumstances resonates outward to the furthest regions of space and then back again.* From a spinner perspective, what each of us experiences here, in this space-time continuum, is limited to four dimensions (height, width, depth and time). This is because there are fine-*grained and gross-grained screens* that cover our senses. These screens are controlled by holodynes and thus everything we experience is limited to our own private event horizon.

Our collective consciousness is limited to our collective event horizon. Once we open an individual event horizon, it expands our conscious awareness as an individual, but it also affects the field dynamics of our collective consciousness. It becomes obvious who we are, what we think and what we do. Our state of being clusters together into various relationships. Everything, even the event horizons of our collective consciousness, is contained within a substructure of consciousness.

This substructure is reflected by the *covenant* we made together. It is hyperspacial and resonates through our Full Potential Self into our microtubules and directly into our holodynes. Thus even our collective pathologies are part of the *covenant.* I like the way Kirk Rector, the great Master Teacher who has accomplished so much in helping the transformation of Russia, demonstrates this in quite an elaborate story about the *covenant*. (See "The Myth of Adoni" in Appendix A.) As the myth suggests, part of the *covenant* contains the promise that we can create change. We can make a difference. Choice exists. Consciousness has impact at ever - expanding levels.

Think about it! Does choice exist? Either it does or it does not. If we believe choice exists, then we can choose!

Since we can choose, we must have chosen everything, for what could we ever experience that we did not choose? Since choice exists, everything in life MUST have been chosen.

By whom? Everything points to the guilty party. Choice is made by those who have choice. So we make the choices. We can choose to shift the field dynamics, change event horizons and transform collective pathologies. We can set our own prime conditions and help others set their prime conditions as well. We can set the prime conditions for groups, systems, and yes, even nations and yes, even for the world.

Once we accept that choice exists, life becomes *part of a team effort*. We can all choose the same thing. As part of a team, we can make *a difference at ever - expanding levels*. Maybe that was the plan all along. We are part of a *covenant*, inseparably connected to those unmanifest dimensions that make up this fantastic reality of the universe. We can access parallel worlds, see into the future, bring it into the now, heal the past and be fully *present* "in the now" as a team.

These processes and this perspective, when applied to the problems of life, provide solutions to every problem. That is the essence of my life work. It is the core discovery of all my testing and research, all my applications of the new sciences to the solutions of our private and collective pathologies and the potentialization of our personal and planetary existence.

We live in a world that is one whole living dynamic - by choice! All Holodynamists understand this and apply it. It changes their view of life. All their fine-grained and gross-grained screens adjust. They experience this world in a different way. They are more conscious of the dynamics, including the field dynamics that are going on around them. They understand the nature of the Covenant and the potential that lies within every set of circumstances. It does not matter which group they join. It does not matter their race, color or creed. They 'get' reality. They know.

Thus Holodynamists tend to create extraordinary results when they choose to focus on unfolding a specific potential. As you team up with other Holodynamists, you will be more empowered to create extraordinary results. So, in this manual, you will be exploring the principles and processes by which you can reach that *state of being* that creates extraordinary results in your own life and within our collective field of consciousness.

These extraordinary results manifest in whatever field your team chooses. It takes focus, alignment with the potential that is to be manifested, teaming up, connecting with the systems associated with the chosen potential, application of principles that drive the solutions and extension of each person's potential into the field. It takes a potentializing process.

Also in this manual, we will be focusing upon actually setting each person's prime conditions and then setting the prime conditions of each team. The ultimate objective is to provide the tools you will need to reach such a state of being that you will naturally team up as manifesters. You will be teaching by action and by word. You naturally become *team teachers* and **Presenters** of Holodynamics. This is the Presenter's Manual.

In Manuals five and six I will outline the principle - driving processes for effective management and how to apply this set of manuals to life projects. In other words, the end result is not just to have your own prime conditions met. It is to have everyone's prime conditions met. This effort is part of the birthing of a new world, a new world order beyond the chaos of the past.

You have heard a lot in the mass media and in private conversations about a new world order. Well, this is not about "that" new world order. This is an alternative new world order. Perhaps, more accurately, this is an alternative or complementary part of a new world order. In this part of the new order, we view the emerging potential coming out of the chaotic conditions of the world. It is a birthing process. The "baby" is this new emerging world order where -

- There is no need for pyramids of power, secret societies or enforced dominance. None are needed because each person understands the nature of their own being. They align with their Full Potential Self and each person chooses the part they will play. Each is self-initiating, self-governing and self-motivated.

- Each person has a stewardship and manifests his or her own potential - by choice;

- Each sets his or her own prime conditions;

- As personal prime conditions are met, each person is free to help others set their prime conditions;

- There is sufficient money for everyone. There is sufficient food, clothing, shelter, energy and living space. No person is excluded;

- It is possible for each person to access those parts of his or her own consciousness that are limiting their potential and to transform these parts into their own potential;

- Each person has the choice to live in harmony within his or her inner world of consciousness. It then becomes possible to live in harmony with family and neighbors. It also becomes possible to become sensitive to all life forms and live a life in balance with nature. We move from competition to cooperation as a collective;

- It becomes possible to provide everyone with high quality education, good information, the ability to communicate with one another and the opportunity to lead productive lives; and

- Using the processes outlined in Holodynamics, we eliminate the need for greed, hoarding and every type of crime or limitation.

You can choose to unleash your magnificent potential and take your place in the potentialization of the planet. It is going to happen with or without you. Why not with you? Why not with all of us? Why not choose now?

At this stage of development, we have organized a team of Holodynamists who can help you establish your Prime Conditions. When you "take the course" (alignment with your Full Potential Self), you will succeed in your prime mission. It is a fact. There are team players who will help you do it.

This world has all the necessary information, resources, people, networks, banking services, even insurance and mortgage capabilities, technologies, new jobs, communication systems and every other thing necessary. Only the holodynes of your Gatekeepers stand in your way.

Everyone qualifies as a candidate. Those who "take the course" qualify as prime candidates whose prime conditions can now be established. That is the purpose of this manual and this course. We intend to help you set your prime conditions. If your prime conditions are already set, we welcome you as a team member. We invite you to help set other people's prime conditions. Let us counsel together, and come to a consensus as to how our individual contributions can combine in such a way as to maximize the rebirth of the planet. Let us choose to shift the field, support a new level of consciousness and spread the power to manifest.

The discoveries of this last century are good news. Consciousness is shifting. The planet is rebirthing a new world. With focus and responsibility, we can each become part of the team that will help unfold the future's greatest potential.

Exercise 6: Commit to your partner and your team members that you will set your prime conditions and help them to set their prime conditions.

Write this commitment in the form of an Agreement. This is a Covenant you make with each other. It is a formal, binding Agreement. This is the business of setting your prime conditions and teaming up with others to set their prime conditions.

In the Agreement, outline the consequences if you fail to perform. Write the conditions of the Agreement as part of the Covenant. Have everyone sign the Agreement. Keep it in a safe place.

Arrange for a review of the conditions of the Agreement at least once a month. Keep track of your performance record. Support one another. Like any team, you agree to work together to score points toward winning the game of setting your prime conditions.

CHAPTER TWO

TEAM BUILDING

W HY *TEAM* BUILDING? BECAUSE EVERY SET OF CIRCUMSTANCES IS DRIVEN BY potential. When you decide to set your prime conditions and you begin to set up certain things to happen (get your home, get it out of mortgage, get a car, etc.), it requires a team. When you decide to accomplish anything, manifest potential of any kind, it requires a team. Why? Because of the Covenant. In order to change, and shift the field, it requires a team who will "covenant" to complete the mission.

The team does not diminish the individual at all. In fact, the team provides an opportunity in which every participant on the team gets to play with the team, and this can be part of the unfolding of more and more of their personal potential. It means that when you are in a team game, a cooperative effort, you must play according to the rules. It does not mean that you have to be defined by or controlled by the rules. You can choose to play another game but you cannot, by agreement, play football on the basketball court when your team has agreed to play basketball.

Exercise 7: Choose your team members. Use the Potentializing Process (Manual I, II and III) as your reference. What do you offer to the team? What skills, information or assets do you have to contribute to the success of the team? Who will be the most valuable player you can choose to help you set your prime conditions? Who is like-minded? Who brings what to the table? How can you decide? Make notes. Begin to design a game plan.

Part of the manifestation of who you are provides you with the opportunity to manifest who you are as a team player. Every technique, from coaching to conflict resolution, contains valuable tools that help with different aspects of teaming up with others. Some great books have been written about team building. It is possible to take a "what works" approach from within the context of Holodynamics and things get really interesting.

When you apply information from a specific approach, no matter which one and you take it into a Holodynamic perspective, it becomes part of the one - whole - dynamic information exchange. Even the Holodynamic approach is limited to its own event horizon. That is, the only way we can each view reality, even as a Holodynamic reality, is through the eyes of the particular event horizon in which we are embedded. We each experience Holodynamics according to our own screens.

Still, one advantage of taking a Holodynamic view is that, by its own definition, it is always open to new event horizons. All systems and all event horizons are all part of one, dynamic universe. We are all involved in an ongoing process. We can't lose anything as individuals by playing on a team. It does not matter which club, church, school, city or nation you belong to. Nothing is ever lost by teaming up with others.

Every approach has some contribution to make and, when you apply that contribution, you will always get better results. You will reap what you sow. Each micro system (person), when incorporated into the larger system, will imbed itself into the team. The team will work only as well as its players. The macro system will work better than the combination of its micro systems when the players are Holodynamic. If the micro systems are not working, the larger system is doomed to certain breakdown. When the people work, the team works. When the team works, the mission works. We manifest success. Things get better and better as time goes on as long as we are each willing to participate in the ever-increasing capacities of new event horizons.

What follows is a brief outline of some successful process used to solve some very complex problems. In fact, before we found solutions, the collective consensus was that these problems "could never be solved." As the solutions became evident, the very people in government institutions who were responsible for the solutions often used the full extent of the law to insure that the very solutions they were responsible to achieve would never be achieved. I soon realized that their resistance was part of the game. Even now, after we have accomplished such remarkable results, some of these same people refuse to admit we solved the problems. I learned from these colleagues and associates that there is no more immovable force than that of an event horizon nestled into someone's comfort zone, held there by fear of success and protected by their own Gatekeepers.

To solve drug abuse threatened those who pushed drugs. The overcoming of addiction threatened those who used addiction to achieve their goals (religious addictions, money addictions and power addictions, for example). The collective field dynamics, fear of the unknown, insecurities, desperate coalitions or divinized pathologies are caused by holodynes held within the collective. Such holodynes can be transformed. Fields can be shifted. It works better when a team gets together and takes action that shifts the field and offers better alternatives.

I hope you can read between the lines because that is where reality can best be experienced. Solutions are found in the realm of being *present*, beyond the frameworks of classical and quantum physics, beyond those fine-grained and gross-grained screens that have been controlling humanity for centuries. Solutions reside within the reservoir of *being* and that is where there are special insights to team building. Here, *between*, you can grasp and own the synergistic power of the mission. You understand the causal potency of each step of the potentialization process. You understand how to track holodynes, shift fields and bring the past and future integrated into the present.

Application of this information and these processes gives you the tools to set your own prime condition and to reach out to help others do the same. Here, in this domain between the worlds, others recognize each team player and we join together in the common cause. Together we can accomplish more than we can accomplish alone. Self-referencing, from between the worlds, and self-organization in this world are the keys that open the door to self-correcting collective action.

Exercise 8: Identify your main mission in life. Outline it in detail.

MY MAIN MISSION IN LIFE (at the present moment) IS:

The way I choose to manifest my Main Mission is as follows (please be specific):

When you are at choice point, free between worlds, every aspect of manifesting your mission, even board meetings, can be fun. Management sessions can be play. Life can be viewed as a self-created experience in which we all decide to play together. It is a state of being *at play*.

In a *particle* mentality, reality is made up of parts. Thus each person is a "part" and each has a vote. It is the sum of the votes that determines the laws and policies that control the whole. Life, in this context, is "serious" business. Every part must conform to the rule of the majority. Every part must survive on its own. Survival is the "basic law of nature."

All particle thinking is superseded by future thought. It is not denied but, more accurately, it is put in its most appropriate place. Linear thinking is used to keep track of things. It is not allowed to lead. It looks at the future as something to be "secured," made safe and planned for as carefully as possible.

The past is used as an example of what did or did not work. Thus, to the rational mind, living in the present means using the past as primary reference while trying to secure a future that is better than the past. The entire system of thought *avoids the present*.

Particle thinkers fail to realize that the only life that can be lived is in the present. One cannot be *present* when one's primary focus is upon the past and future. There are no solutions to anything within this mentality.

In a *quantum* world, the *sum of the parts* are superseded by *the whole*. The whole itself becomes, as in Communism, the final determinant. Individual rights, human rights, the right to information, protection under law, participation and even an individual vote are all secondary to the identity of the state.

The assumption is that herd mentality, swarm intelligence and flock dynamics insure a better chance of survival. The contribution of collective thought is that it moves beyond linear and into nonlinear consciousness. Whether you agree or not with this idea, the goal is still the same. The goal is survival. "Survival of the species takes precedence over survival of the individual." The team is treated as though it were an individual. Society becomes one team against all other teams, one country or group of countries, against all other countries. One victory is a victory of the whole. To win an Olympic event brings pride to every individual. It is still the survival mentality, still win - lose and still "us" against "them" and there are no solutions to anything within this mentality.

These two points of view, particle and wave, are byproducts of two types of thinking: rational and emotional. One is linear and the other nonlinear, but they stem from the same assumption. They both assume that the primary directive is to survive! Each has a different group of assumptions that stem from this one, singular assumption.

On the surface, each point of view seems inalterably opposite from the other. Masculine/feminine, head versus heart, divine versus materialism, and who shall control - democracy or communism - to insure survival. *Hot* and *cold* wars have been fought over this apparent dichotomy. Each seems to be an irreconcilable different philosophy. They seem irreconcilable because solutions cannot be found in either a particle or wave mentality. Neither "side" will ever win. <u>Neither side *can* ever win</u>. It is a lose - lose game because neither side takes into account the whole dynamic.

In a Holodynamic universe, the parts and the whole are both important. They give content and context to the dynamics of life. The sum of the whole is much greater than the sum of the parts. Why? Because both the *parts* and the *whole* are *conscious*. Particle thinking provides for the accounting of content but does not allow for context. Wave thinking allows for context but does not allow for the infusion of will.

Only in a conscious universe can one be fully conscious, and only when one is fully conscious can one discover the power of will, the impact of choice and the meaning of life. To remain at choice point is to remain free. At "choice point" you can find the solutions to every problem. Consciousness is an embracive superposition.

To choose, by the presence of one's own will, and to accomplish an objective is to create a result that appears as if by magic to those who do not understand the nature of the Holodynamic universe. If there is any magic at all, it is the fact that everything is magic. We are here by choice and we function by choice. What choice? The choice inherent within our natures, within our Full Potential Selves: the choice to unfold potential.

Once aware of your Full Potential Self, you have the freedom to choose. You can use your Full Potential Self as your "source," as an individual, to make the distinctions, sense more clearly your options, empower your creativity, join a team of like-minded people and create the magic of a mission.

The Magic of the Mission

There is magic to the mission - an unfolding of emerging potential as powerful as any driving life force. It creates its own vortex. Like the root of a tree that can crack solid rock and lift entire highways in its path, nothing can stop the mission when it is held by each individual and by a team that is aligned with their fullest potential, focused and functioning in harmony with each other. They are empowered. Team building within the magic of a mission is one of the most passionate, invigorating and satisfying activities in life.

To free ourselves from the event horizons that hold us confined from our potential, consider some of the differences between the particle, wave and Holodynamic views of reality.

Consider, for example, the chart that follows.

Exercise 9: Review through the various subjects as they are presented in the chart on particle, wave and Holodynamic thinking.

Discuss with your team the applications of this information in your team mission. Make notes.

PARTICLE THINKING	WAVE THINKING	HOLODYNAMIC THINKING
Newtonian physics	Quantum physics	Holodynamic physics
Simple	Complex	Embracing
Law-abiding	Chaotic	Purposeful
Control-oriented	Go with the flow	Coherent
Atomism	Holism	Potential - driven choices
Emphasis on separate parts	Emphasis on relationships	Emphasis on self-organizing information systems
Fragmented	Dynamic	Integrative
Determinate	Indeterminate	Omnipresent
Values certainty and predict-ability	Adaptable to uncertainty and ambiguity	Creative
Regimented	Loosely adhering	Intelligent
Reductive	Inductive	Emergent
Isolated content - focused	Contextual	Self-organizing
Self-referenced	Group-referenced	Conscious reality-referenced
Parts rule the whole	Whole rules parts	Dynamic Interactive Collaboration
Top - down management	Grass Roots Management	Leadership by Intention
Driven by individual goals	Driven by group goals	Covenant - driven correlation
Reactive	Experiential	Imaginative - proactive

Exercise 9 (continued): What team perspective do you choose?

Discuss the characteristics of teams that are organized around each of the three systems of information and three types of leadership consciousness listed above. Make notes.

Exercise 10: Creative Work of Art

Organize into teams of six people.. Provide each team with an ample supply of Playdoh in various colors. Instruct each team that this is a competition. Each person must make a work of art.

Instruct the groups that their team must decide whose work of art is the best. That one is chosen will join with the whole group for the next level of competition. The group must decide whose is <u>best</u> in the whole group. One more rule - N<u>o one can lose</u>.

Allow time for each group to choose the best without anyone losing. After they have figured it out (all members of the team combine theirs so the combination is "best" and no one loses), the entire group will combine it work together.

After they have had time to marvel at their creation, have someone come in and destroy the entire work of art.

Discuss participant's reactions to the destruction of their work of art. What reference do they use to express themselves? (Use the Mind Model as your reference to look at their reference framework).

Actuality versus Mathematical Probabilities versus Potentiality

Business in a Western culture runs mainly on linear thinking. In classical physics, the concern was with the here and now. This view is based on the limited assumption that "reality is to be found in things one can see and touch and measure." The focus is on "actuality" as a "true description" of our four-dimensional, space-time continuum.

This limited view is supported by the development of the Industrial Revolution, rapid growth of technology and the Information Age. In a more expanded view of reality, linear thinking has marketed itself well in the West. Linear thinking has taken credit for almost every advancement in society. As a result, this type of thinking has developed deep roots as an internal state of *consensus*. It burns deeply into our thinking and our religious beliefs and controls the way we worship, educate our youth, govern our country and do business. The result is that our view of reality has become described as *valid* when it is linear and rational.

In Russia, China and other "common - ism" countries, thinking has developed on a more nonlinear basis. All Russian scientists, for example, have been taught quantum physics is the basis of reality. This has been going on for almost half a century. Whereas, in Western society, quantum physics is only taught to a minority of physicists even today. Quantum science moved beyond the linear actuality into the mathematical probabilities that were demonstrably causal in physical systems. Reality, these quantum thinkers suggest, lays hidden beyond our grasp, indefinably. It is yet to unfold; it cannot be computed. It exists as a series of probabilities.

This view is also supported by an internal state of being. Information self-organizes into nonlinear systems that flow with emotion and intuition. Team efforts, group consensus and community are natural and easy in such societies. Like swarm intelligence among insects, fish and birds, or herd instincts among mammals, societies take on collective consciousness. These people think and act based upon probabilities, consensus and group pride. Business is mainly a "good old boy" association.

In Holodynamics, we talk about potentiality. It is the most difficult concept for people in our culture to grasp and yet it's the closest thing to us. We are potentializers. We think and create from a state of being aware of the potential that exists within the implicate order of the potential fields making up our reality. We are capable of being linear and nonlinear at the same time. We are also capable of being causal and creative, as well as teaming up to accomplish our objectives. We do this all at the same time. Businesses, teams, groups, communities and societies take on a very different form when their minds have become aware of the whole dynamic.

Business, or any project or organization, for example, is about emerging potential according to an implicate order. The **Bird's-Eye View Chart of Business Development Dynamics,** found later in this section, is an example of putting form and structure around market - driven potential. It creates a dynamic perspective regarding business.

The linear thinker reasons, "Well, facts are, after all, facts. Let's stick to them." It is the ideas that, if you can get something in your hand, eat it. Use it and have it as a resource. Then this is worth more than anything else - hypothetically or theoretically. Therefore, we trust the substance scientist. We trust the particle thinker because his facts are in front of our eyes and all our fine-grained/gross-grained screens are already adjusted to it. We are "in the covenant" of a particle world. Therefore, we trust substances. We can capture them in test tubes. We can analyze them. We can describe them on graphs. We can get Cartesian coordinates, give geometric dimensions to them and begin to predict. We become Newtonian/Copernican team players.

We all agree that we will just stick to the facts and we trust the results. We have employers and employees. We can see the paper shuffle. We can see the people move. Therefore, we know the number of hours they put on the job is measurable and, therefore, the job must be being done. If people do not perform according to predictions, we set up pyramids of power and enforce restrictions or impose more regulations until performance meets our expectations. It does not work, but we give our pyramids the credit for what is working. We just do not know what is working. It is amazing that, within this framework, anything is working.

Then come the quantum thinkers. The quantum thinker does his most creative thinking "in abstractions" when his mind is not busy. He wants time off from all the ritual and regimentation of work.

When he concentrates on a particular mental task, the quantum thinker will want to look at the energy involved in that task. Understanding the energy is effective for achieving the goal in sight, but he resists the fragmentation of linear thinking. The quantum thinker wants more freedom to be able to be nonlinear, more freedom to extend down into some insight and some inner knowing about the broader perspective. Therefore, he wants a gut - level feeling about what is going on. Those who meditate (usually on the "spiritual" end of the quantum wave) will go into an altered state or what they call "zero point," where they think nothing, become nothing, and get rid of all of the linear aspects. This search for freedom ends in the same type of event horizon as does the linear system of thought. The quantum thinker becomes immersed in the wave of his own undulation.

Both positions are a polarization. It is usually linear *against* nonlinear in order to gain a grasp on reality and/or nonlinear *against* the linear in order to obtain a more inclusive interactive state.

In the quantum case, you would relax, get up from your desk, move away, go get a drink down at the fountain, look out the window and just think nothing. Suddenly it is as if the problem will solve itself. It is as though out of the wave dynamic is supposed to spontaneously emerge the specific solution. Usually you (the quantum thinker) will have no theory for how this works except that awareness somehow makes contact with the ground state or full potential of consciousness.

Quantum thinkers have no science with which to explain the full potential of consciousness. You might contend that within the quantum field is this full potential of consciousness. Rather than creating a science about the full potential of consciousness, you would likely insist it has a wave dynamic of some kind and, therefore, it comes out of one of the many, infinite possibilities of potential.

The contribution of quantum science is to realize that when you try to measure any specific activity, you can only measure from the sense of actually being part of it. Therefore, you influence it as part of the measurement. It is like a giant picking up your car to see what is inside and then concluding that the little people are always screaming. They insist, as Hiesenburg does with his Uncertainty Principle, that anything that we can say about a quantum system is only part of the story. Facts are not just facts. You cannot measure the weight of a running horse. You cannot know location and mass at the same time.

It is necessary, if one expects to maximize potential of a team, to acknowledge that our understanding depends upon how we look at the facts, upon what questions we have asked in arriving at them, and upon what value we place on them.

As soon as we place a value on the facts, we change our perspective about the facts. Our screens shift so that our particular reality becomes aligned with our particular focus. We create our own reality simply by confining it to a single event horizon.

In *The Dance of Life,* we go into detail about linear, nonlinear and Holodynamic consciousness. We explore many games showing the distinction between three kinds of thinking and three kinds of dynamics. When we team up to play a specific game, we had best be aware that all games, all interactions, all physical reality interact according to these three basic information systems: particle (linear, rational), wave (nonlinear, emotional) and presence (intelligent, creative).

There is also an advantage to understanding the way we relate and about the nature of ourselves, when we realize we originate in spinner form. Everything is information in motion. Some games go according to the linear lines of the spinner effect and some go according to the wave dynamics, while other information flows according to conscious creation. While the whole organization of the information system is constantly interweaving itself, those who are creative are able to influence the pattern of the whole dynamic.

So, the finite thinker is someone who plays the game *by* the rules perspective and sets goals and objectives. The infinite game player is someone who plays *with* the rules and goes with the flow and whose only objective is to continue the game. However, the Holodynamist understands both the finite and infinite games and the different rules and then *sets* his own game to manifest potential. That is, the Holodynamist can enter the game from a position of being *present* from all positions at once and thus focus upon the potential he chooses and create in spite of the game. A Holodynamist *makes the rules* and uses the game to manifest potential.

The mission for Holodynamists is to "take the course" and inspire others to do the same. It is about how to potentialize your life. "Taking the course" is about potentializing every set of circumstances on which you choose to focus. It is to help people join, and "stay on course" so that each person, family, group, community and nation can be potentialized.

Exercise 11: Review your Main Mission Statement

Is it rationally based? Is it emotionally based? In what ways is it Holodynamic? How does it align with your Full Potential Self? Ask your Full Potential Self about your life mission. Write down any changes or clarifications your Full Potential Self suggests regarding your Main Mission in life.

A Bird's-Eye View

Following this page is a chart I have called the **Bird's-Eye View Chart of Business Development Dynamics.** This chart takes the six levels of development and applies them to each dimension of a normal business. It also applies to any project and can be helpful in guiding you to set your prime conditions.

Exercise 12: Review the Bird's-Eye View Chart.

After you have reviewed the chart, discuss with your team how this chart might be utilized to evaluate manifesting your Main Mission as a project.

For example, assuming that the manifesting of your Main Mission takes place as a process, where are you now in the process? What has already manifested? What has yet to manifest? Make notes.

Exercise 13: Pay the Game

In this exercise, each person receives a decided - upon number of $1 bills (Monopoly money can also be used). Each team receives an equal number of dollars. These are divided equally among the members of the team.

Each participant chooses his or her own project. They work out a prospectus or presentation of their project. When everyone is ready, each participant takes two minutes and presents the main idea and mission of the project. As the presentations are made, team players can choose to "invest" their dollars in another team player's project.

When all projects have been presented to the team, the team must decide which project they choose to support. All money then goes into that project and the team must then decide who will be the presenter of that project to the larger group.

The process is repeated in the larger group. Each presenter has two minutes to convince the group their project should have its prime conditions set. The team captain of each group (the one who presents) then consults with each group to decide where their dollars shall be invested.

A general discussion is held to summarize what happened.

> *Was the project practical? Would it work?*
> *How did you feel when your project was not the winning project?*
> *What holodynes did it raise for you?*
> *How did you manage the holodynes (if any)?*
> *Did you identify any potential team players for your own project?*
> *What do you want to do about it?*

Note that the Business Development Dynamics chart (which provides "a Bird's-eye View") outlines the stages of development for creating and running a business.

In order to read the chart sequentially you will want to begin at the bottom of the chart on the left-hand side with the section titled: "Physical." Then read upward to the section titled: "Identity" and then to "Communications," "Systems," "Quality" and "Market Integration." Each of these sections follows a natural built-in order of development from the simple to the complex.

Note also that the major departments within a corporation are listed: Management, Administration, Human Resources, Research and Development, Operations, Finance and Accounting, Public Relations/Marketing and Sales. Each department has a natural order of development. In order to read the department in a sequential order, begin at the bottom of the column and read upward from "Physical" (the bottom A-1) to "Identity" (A-2) and on upward through each section under "Management." This same approach applies to each department.

Bird's-Eye View Chart of Business Development Dynamics

BUSINESS DEVELOP

UP-DRAFT DYNAMICS	Management	Administration	Human Resources
Market Integration **To Integrate** Are we in alignment with our mission statement & up-to-date in our specialty? Are we open to change & ready to respond? *(Stage 6)*	Review/redefine company mission statement to ensure alignment with company & marketplace potential. Optimum contribution to marketplace. Aware of changes in management styles & trends. Open to change and demonstrates leadership. **A-6**	Aligned with company mission, vision & values. Aware & responsive to changes in marketplace affecting administrative services. Open to implementing change. **B-6**	Aligned with company mission, vision & values. Aware & responsive to changes in human resources marketplace. Open to implementing change. **C-6**
Quality **To Evaluate** Are we doing what we set out to do? Is our production/service in alignment with our qualities & standards? *(Stage 5)*	Company is meeting needs of all participants/stakeholders. Operating in accordance with statutory & regulation laws. Compliant with company principles & standards. Operating according to plan & at potential. **A-5**	Company is supported by appropriate level of administrative services. Procurement practices reflect demographic & environmental sensitivities. **B-5**	Staff follows & upholds all policies, rules & procedures. Performance expectations are met & employees recognized. Compliant with current human resource laws, standards & basic human rights. **C-5**
Systems **To Support** What systems are needed to support us in reaching our goal? What can be done to have all the parts work together? *(Stage 4)*	Integrated management information systems developed & maintained. All departments work together. Adequate management expertise available/accessible. **A-4**	All company & marketplace interaction & procedures are facilitated with order & cooperation. **B-4**	Open & effective staff selection & training. Maintain & facilitate healthy team dynamics. **C-4**
Communications **To Connect** Who do we need to connect with? What methods & styles of communication would best serve our purpose? *(Stage 3)*	Regular meetings set for contingency planning, information evaluation & dissemination among all levels of management. Information flows freely between management, the "field" & the marketplace. **A-3**	Communications maintain commitment/accountability. Communications are timely, appropriate & effective. General meetings & events are effective. Policies & procedures are written & distributed. **B-3**	Communications are open, honest & effective. Employee related reports & information are distributed. Employee morale is monitored & supported. Policies & procedures are written & distributed. **C-3**
Identity **To Define** What are we about? What is the job/task/purpose that needs to be fulfilled? *(Stage 2)*	Company mission, vision & values reflect potential. Cooperate culture envisioned. Goals & strategic objectives defined. **A-2**	Establish administrative support expectations, service levels, responsibilities & guidelines. Develop procurement policies & procedures. **B-2**	Develop job descriptions/responsibilities/expectations. Develop performance management program. Design HR development training goals & guidelines. Develop HR policies. **C-2**
Physical **To Establish** What do we want? What do we need to get the job done? *(Stage 1)*	Establish legal entity & ownership agreements. Develop business plan. Obtain licenses & certifications. **A-1**	Obtain/install office furniture, equipment, stationary & supplies. Establish office space, file systems, mail processing & procurement functions. **B-1**	Develop organizational structure. Develop flexible employee benefit program. Develop compensation plan based on open labor market. **C-1**

The International Academy of Holodynamics uses this Business Development Dynamics approach as a tool in teaching corporate leaders some of the basic information about business. Whether you are just starting to organize a new business or your business is a long-established and successful business, the development dynamics are vital to your continued success. Whether you are in the manufacturing business or in the rendering of services business, your business is about potentializing.

...MENT DYNAMICS

Research & Development	Operations	Finance & Accounting	Marketing/Sales Public Relations
Aligned with company mission, vision & values. Aware of new products & services in marketplace. Anticipate potential of new technologies and innovations. **D-6**	Aligned with company mission, vision & values. Aware of new technologies & changes in the production /service marketplace. Open to changes in production & service processes & delivery. **E-6**	Aligned with company mission, vision & values. Aware & responsive to financial marketplace changes. Able to forecast impacts of change. **F-6**	Aligned with company mission, vision & values. Aware of changes in specific product/service marketplace. Achieving market potential. Open to what is wanted & needed next. **G-6**
Product /service meeting ideal product/service standards & purpose. Compliant with environmental & regulatory laws. **D-5**	Workplace is safe & healthy. Product/service preparation/delivery are compliant with environmental/green laws. Product specifications are met. Q&M standards met. Production quotas/standards are met. **E-5**	Books, records & reports are "clean". Information is disclosed in full compliance with current financial rules/regulations. Financial goals are reviewed & updated regularly. **F-5**	Sales/marketing/PR strategy is on target with goals & effective in marketplace. Sales methods are "clean", honest, straight & effective. Customer ethics, policies & guidelines upheld. **G-5**
Source development. Product specification. Product production planning. **D-4**	Product manufactured. Product/service distributed. Orders processed. Customers serviced. **E-4**	Adequate control systems throughout company. Record keeping & forecasting is accurate, timely & meaningful. Report distribution allows full accountability, knowledge & openness. **F-4**	Customer contracts monitored. Effectiveness of marketing & sales communications tracked & evaluated. Marketplace & customer relations maintained. **G-4**
Ongoing testing & evaluation performed inside & outside company. Products/service redesigned/developed via feedback. **D-3**	Product/service & provider is clearly understood. Production/service planning schedules are maintained. Subcontractor/supplier agreements are in place. Policies & procedures are written & distributed. **E-3**	Profitability alignment reviewed regularly. Healthy ongoing financial relationships maintained. Reports published. Healthy vendor relations. Policies & procedures are written & distributed. **F-3**	Production/service presentation established. Sales, promotional copy & materials written & distributed. Product/services sold. Sales reports distributed. **G-3**
Define product/service purpose. Define ideal performance & use of product/service. Define ideal product/service standards. **D-2**	Establish detailed flow of production/service operations. Establish production/service costs & pricing. Establish productivity & performance standards. **E-2**	Establish profitability standards. Define record keeping parameters. Establish priorities, deadlines & report types. **F-2**	Develop sales, marketing & public relation strategy & goals. Develop product/service identity. **G-2**
Design & build prototype. **D-1**	Establish production area, processes & procedures. Obtain/install production/service equipment. Arrange for raw materials/resources. **E-1**	Establish banking & finance relationships. Develop budgets & forecasts. Establish risk management. Forecast cash & capital requirements. **F-1**	Identify & target customer profile. Prepare market research. Design product packaging. **G-1**

Chapter Three

The Potentialization Process

THE POTENTIALIZATION PROCESS BEGINS WITH FOCUS. WHAT MISSION OR POTENTIAL you choose and what you want to unfold will depend upon how well you align with your Full Potential Self. In turn, the clarity you experience with your Full Potential Self will depend upon how well you potentialize your holodynes, as well as how well you enroll others, form teams, build the system and stay attuned to principle - driving processes. As you penetrate the field dynamics of the larger society, how you manage your life, relationships, team dedication and collective fields determines the extent to which you are successful.

This is not about being a success or being a failure. This is about you. It is about you choosing to manifest your own dreams. It is about you making a difference in the world. It is about you being able to manifest your own potential at every level of development and in all dimensions of reality. Everyone is already successful. Just getting here makes each person a champion. Why are we here? We are here to potentialize or, in other words, to manifest potential. Why are we drawn together? We are here together because of the field dynamics that embed us with one another so we could potentialize our relationships. As we potentialize our relationships we potentialize field dynamics.

One of the tools of potentialization is the Mind Model. Use the Mind Model every step of the way. I will explain some of the ways this can be done as we go briefly through the steps of potentialization.

Exercise 14: Review the Six Stages of Potentializing Chart (see Manual I and II) and each of the steps.

Discuss with your team how to move from step to step and why each step is necessary and natural in the process of potentializing.

Discuss how you can do this as a team in the process of reaching your mission goals.

Life is about potentializing. Your unique personal potential begins in hyperspace as your Full Potential Self.

You begin to manifest in this space-time continuum as a specific DNA code that emerges from the quantum potential field within the microtubules of the combined sperm and egg of your parents.

From multiple dimensions you form into spinners of information that provide the codes for your cellular organization and create the microtubules that make up the walls of your cells. Your microtubules provide the necessary environment for the formation of your holodynes that create the formation of your body in the womb.

You are born, develop personality and progress through various stages during your life. You are nurtured within an intimate family, join with a community, develop a profession, and adapt to principles that give meaning to your life. Eventually you embrace reality and accept your place in the universal state of being present. In chart form, it looks like this:

LIFE IS ONE WHOLE DYNAMIC HARMONIC

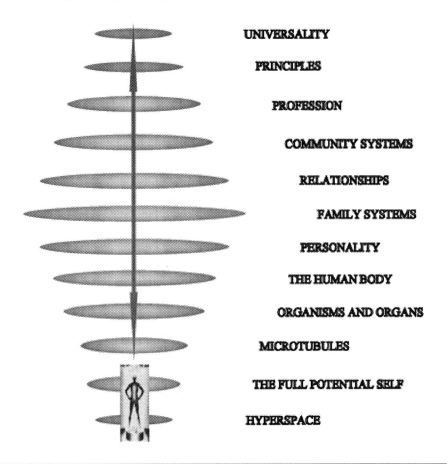

UNIVERSALITY

PRINCIPLES

PROFESSION

COMMUNITY SYSTEMS

RELATIONSHIPS

FAMILY SYSTEMS

PERSONALITY

THE HUMAN BODY

ORGANISMS AND ORGANS

MICROTUBULES

THE FULL POTENTIAL SELF

HYPERSPACE

From hyperspace, your Full Potential Self is continually orchestrating a harmonic information field that resonates through your microtubules and into the organs of your body. This gives your body coherence and provides an environment for your personality. This same harmonic resonates through your relationships, family and community, including your workplace. The entire harmonic is principle-driven and part of a larger, universal field that is woven together by covenant. We all agreed to be part of the unfolding of our potential. We unfold potential together.

FOCUS

Focus is the *willful decision to put your attention on a specific objective.* Once you focus, your fine-grained and gross-grained screens adjust and reality responds. If it does not respond, you have not focused clearly or you have not followed through on your focus. Most people who do not get what they want either do not know what they want or they do not know how to focus on it with the power to manifest. There are tools that can further assist you in making clear your focus and unfolding its potential. Here is one tool:

SIX STAGES OF POTENTIALIZING

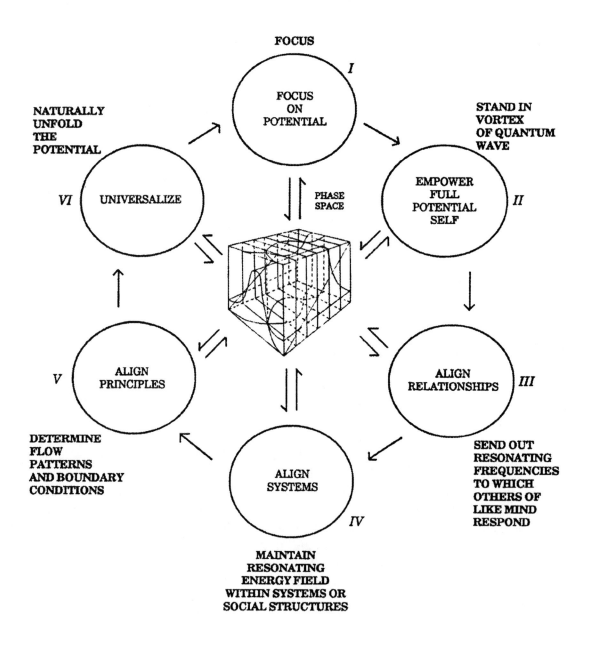

We have discussed how to use the Six Stages of Potentialization for transforming holo-dynes and relationships. Understanding the natural stages through which an organization grows can be very helpful when you want to focus on what your team wants. Here are some sugges-tions.

Notice that a central part of the Potentializing process is the Mind Model. You can use the Mind Model in your focusing process. You may find it helpful to ask the following ques-tions:

1. Is my focus rational or emotional? Is it reasonable? Does it feel right?

Remember, there are no solutions to particle and wave thinking. Solutions are found when you are in that state of *being* the solution. You will not get what you want or potentialize anything if all you do is think and feel it. You must "become" the potential and let it manifest itself through you.

How do you reach that state of being? Even those who know how to focus must first potentialize their holodynes because they realize their holodynes are usually in control of their focus. One of the problems we all face is that our focus is contaminated by immature and dys-functional holodynes.

2. What holodynes, including family and/or cultural holodynes, are influencing my focus?

Accessing your holodynes and potentializing them frees you from their control. In fact, it uses the energy that once resisted solutions *in* the potentializing process.

3. What level of development am I functioning from when I focus?

You must know what you want in spite of all the other information systems around you. As a unique entity, you have the inherent right to assert your own special "fingerprint" upon the field. That is, your "fingerprint" stands for the unique aspects of yourself that are manifesting in this world. When you are operating from a mentality or from holodynes that are not aligned with your Full Potential Self, the interference can "derail your prosperity train."

Immature holodynes create inappropriate focus. By inappropriate I mean focusing upon a personal dynamic (like the color of someone's eyes, for example) when the team is focused upon a group dynamic (who will be responsible for preparing a systems analysis of the structure necessary to complete a job). Mis - focus can create endless drama, distraction and war games. Most people do not even realize they are creating the problem.

Once you step back and observe yourself and your holodynes, you can establish a more conscious awareness of where you are in your own development. You realize you are at a cer-tain level of awareness and the next natural step is to arrange to take that step forward. This requires that you transform your holodynes, establish the level of development from which you choose to function and even do it with the support of a team. It may not be the team you are working with, but it will be a team who knows how to coach you in getting into that state of being that you need to do the job. They will coach you until you become a professional at accomplishing your part of the team mission.

4. Do I have any comfort zone dynamics that limit the team effort?

One of the great values of teaming up is the feedback other team members provide. They sense things you cannot sense. They cover your back and help you see through your blinders. Teaming up with people who are not "yes" people about such things can be uncomfortable, but it can be well worth it in the long run. Especially when the communication is clear, focused and delivered with positive intent.

5. Am I dedicated to devote energy - plus to this project?

It takes dedication and energy to accomplish goals worthy of your focus. I am not saying the job is hard or should be a struggle. Hardship and struggle are holodynes. Dedication, on the other hand, means to focus your energy in sufficient amounts to get the job done. There is no way to measure this directly but there is a knowing about your own dedication to manifest what is wanted. Results will follow.

6. Am I able to integrate this information at the next level of potentialization?

Now that your focus is clear, can you, for example, take the information you have created toward focus, and dedicate it to the next step? What next step?

If you follow the chart on Potentializing, you will note that you move from focus to referencing your Full Potential Self. What this means is that you check every decision made so far through your Full Potential Self. Does your Full Potential Self agree with you about your focus? Are you aligned? Do your partners agree? Does your Being of Togetherness (BOT)? Does the team agree? Does the team Being of System Synergy (BOSS) agree? You will be amazed at how empowered your projects can become when aligned with everyone's fullest potential and with the fullest potential of the project.

You want, for example, to establish your personal prime conditions? So you establish your Prime Condition by knowing what you want, and then by focusing upon it from that state of being at your fullest potential. You then plan it by taking it trough the potentializing process.

Exercise 15: Using the Mind Model, identify what you consider to be the essentials of what you want in order to set your Prime Conditions.

List these essentials and discuss each essential with your team. Do they agree? Or not agree? Do others have suggestions that might be of value to you in setting your Prime Conditions?

At what stage of development is your project? Discuss with your team. What is the next stage?

Aligning with Full Potential Self

After you have identified what you want, the next stage is for you to check with your Full Potential Self. This becomes part of how you start each day. You ask your Full Potential Self what activities are to be done today that will unfold the potential of your team. Make this a **day-start** and **day - close** exercise as part of your routine.

If you have not already done so, create a Place of Peace in your mind. This is a place (imaginary or real) in which you feel at peace. In your Place of Peace create a Round Table at which you can meet. Invite your Full Potential Self to meet you there. Hold regular meetings. Check in with your Full Potential Self at the beginning of the day and find out what is wanted this day. At the end of the day (and as many times as you like during the day), check back in. Ask your Full Potential Self how well you did in accomplishing the mission of unfolding your fullest potential. Keep notes. Organize your mind so it responds to the discipline of conscious action.

Part of the discipline is to regularly run your agreement (with your Full Potential Self) through the various aspects of the Mind Model. Do you both agree it is reasonable, honorable, feels right, is at the most mature level of development possible, and that all holodynes from your family and society are aligned with your objectives? If any holodynes are not aligned you can Track and potentialize them. If you do not know how to Track, review the section on Tracking in the Appendix or get an experienced Consultant to help you learn the process.

Once your Full Potential Self agrees on your mission, you can focus on the next step. If any holodynes try to take over, Track them and transform them so they are aligned with your objectives. Now putting the time, energy and work into reaching your objectives is easy. Seldom will you get tired and never will you get bored.

Exercise 16: List below any resistance you meet to fulfilling your mission. Cluster the dynamics surrounding the resistance. Track the holodynes involved and keep a record.

Enrolling the Team

Since everything is in relationship, there will be people who share similar missions and have similar objectives and who are willing to put their time, energy and resources into the project. As you send out a clear message, people will respond, and you will find all the support you need coming to your assistance. If you are not getting support, you must find out why.

- Use the Mind Model and look at the whole dynamic.
- Check in with your Full Potential Self. Ask who to contact next.
- Reach out. Deal with people Full Potential to Full Potential.

- Follow the lead given by your Full Potential Self.
- Take the course of the BOT and the BOSS.
- Make sure that everyone agrees to the principles that drive your team effort.
- Extend it systematically into the world.

Make sure the team is enrolled and that everyone knows their part.

Develop a time management program. At the beginning of each day, ask your Full Potential Self: "What would you like me to accomplish this day?" Make a schedule of events that lead to accomplishing what is wanted. Keep track, make appointments, manifest every aspect of the job and get it done.

Team up with others of like mind. You will relate to others in the same way your holodynes relate to each other. Learn to listen to your own internal dialogues. Access the holodynes; potentialize the Being of Togetherness among them. Reach out and form a Being of Togetherness (Manual Three) with each of the people on the team. As part of your day-start program, call upon the BOT you have developed with each person. Ask what is wanted this day to meet the objectives and align with the potential of the BOT with your key team members. Make lists. Schedule tasks. Take responsibility. Allow your state of being to become the BOT. Align your actions accordingly. At day close, check in. Make sure you note those tasks that still need to be done in order to reach the fullest potential of each BOT.

Develop purposeful relationships. Meet together regularly. Plan together how to reach your fullest potential as a team. What do you have in common? What do you all want? How can you help each other reach your common goals? Outline the tasks, who has responsibility and what bench marks will indicate you are on target with your goals.

Take time to sense the Being of Systems Synergy (BOSS) that develops among the team. Align with the fullest potential of the BOSS. As part of your day-start program, call upon the BOSS you have developed with the team. Ask what is wanted this day to meet the objectives and align with the potential of the BOSS along with your key team members. Make lists. Schedule tasks. Take responsibility. Allow your state of being to become the BOSS. Align your actions accordingly. At day close, check in. Make sure you note those tasks that still need to be done in order to reach the fullest potential of your BOSS.

Exercise 17: Time Management

If you have not already done so, develop a time management system for the entire team. Daily planners usually will do the job. Computer - based time management schedules also work for those who have daily access to computers. Daily appointments, task outlines, phone numbers, e-mail addresses and discussion groups, phone and other forms of communication networks can be planned for, developed and implemented as part of the best use of one's time in relationship to the team and the job.

Review the time management system you are currently using with your team.

Building the System

The potential for the system already exists. When you step out, joined by those who are your team players, and declare you are going to put structure around the team and the manifestation of the potential, the entire field responds. You must understand the nature of the society in which you are birthing your system. You must understand the rules, regulations, and function of each aspect of the system. You must give it *form* and that form must fit within the system. In the sections that follow, the giving of form and the nature of function will be discussed. Use the Mind Model and the six - level **Bird's-Eye View** management chart as your guide.

Exercise 18: Review the Bird's-Eye View Chart. Use it as a project management guide. Whether you are just starting to build a system, or whether your team is working with one already in existence, use the chart to evaluate the current potential of the system. Discuss with the team and make notes below. For example:

1. *What is the main mission of the program?*
2. *Do you, at your fullest potential, agree with this mission?*
3. *Can you identify others who agree? What does each person bring to the table that will contribute to the mission?*
4. *What other resources will you require? Can you locate them? Who will be responsible for what?*
5. *What principles guide your team?*
6. *When the project is finished and all aspects of it are manifest, does it work in the world?*

Using the chart, answer the questions at each level beginning from the bottom and working to the top of the chart.

Have you established an identity, given it form, a name and a clear statement of purpose?

Have you clarified what communication channels are necessary to serve your purpose?

Work your way through the chart as a team. Identify each area that has already been accomplished and check it off. Identify which areas are under development and who is responsible for their completion. Identify those areas that have yet to be addressed. Choose a time and place to address each area and propose an approximate completion time.

Once an area of potential development is identified, review that area with team members. Make sure the potential is clearly understood. Discuss with team member: Who is willing and qualified to take responsibility for reaching the goal? Take notes. Use your daily planners. Take action. Report in and keep the activities and progress working according to benchmarks. Benchmarks indicate progress made so the team is aware of everything happening.

As one goal is reached, move on to the next. Never use past successes to fortify future promises. Use only the moment to express your own personal presence so that everything possible is manifest now. Make notes, keep track and process any resistance.

MY TIME MANAGEMENT PROCEDURES ARE AS FOLLOWS:

_____

_____

_____

_____

_____

_____

_____

_____

_____

_____

_____

_____

_____

Principle-driven Processes

Are you willing to operate based on *always* making "the best deal possible"? Does the team agree, for example, that they will only do business if it is the best deal possible for everyone on the team and anyone with whom you are dealing? Using the Mind Model, it is easy and natural to find *the best deal possible*. The best deal possible would not allow anyone to lose. It would be a win - win deal. It would not be damaging to others or to the environment. It would not sacrifice anyone for the system but would find a way to include everyone. It would be internally and externally integritous. We will discuss in detail some of the principle-driven processes in the next manual.

Exercise 19: Orange Grove

Have participants number off one, two and three. This divides the group into three equal groups. Have all the Number - One people go to one corner of the room, the Number - Two people go to another, separate corner and the Number - Three people to a third corner. Give private instructions to each group.

To Number - One People: You each own an orange grove. You produce a "grove" of oranges each year. The fair market value of your oranges is $50,000 cash. Your assignment, though, is to go into the open market and "make the best deal possible."

To Number - Two People: You each own an orange - peel factory. You take the peels off oranges and make them into expensive oils, candies and other exotic things. Your assignment is to go into the open market and purchase the peels from a grove of oranges. The fair market value of a grove of orange peels is $25,000 cash. You have the cash, and your assignment is to get "the best deal possible" in the open market.

To Number - Three People: You each own an orange - juice company. You take the inside of the oranges - the pulp - and squeeze it into juice concentrate. Your assignment is to go into the open market and purchase the pulp from a grove of oranges. The fair market value of a grove of pulp is $25,000. You have this money in cash, but your assignment is to get out there in the open market and "make the best deal possible."

The Facilitator then announces to the entire group: "Will all the "One's" hold up one finger. All the "Two's" hold up two fingers and all the "Three's" hold up three fingers. Get together with a One, a Two and a Three and let's make a deal!"

This is a simple transaction. The only thing to figure out is that 25 plus 25 equals 50. Still, it is amazing to observe the holodynes that come into play. After about ten to fifteen minutes, close the marketplace and have each team report on what happened. Did they make "the best deal possible?" Did they make a deal in which everyone was a winner or did they let their partners lose money? Did they keep things simple and relationships clear or did they set up co-ops, wheel and deal sharing businesses and creating unnecessary structures or alliances? Were they "sharks" or were they "carps" to be eaten?

Exercise 20: Money Circle

Have participants form into a large circle. If there are more than 40 people, have them form into multiple circles of no more than 40 people.

Have each person get a "greenback" - some denomination of money with the admonition that the money is "at risk." Each person should have someone on their left and someone on their right. The Facilitator then instructs: "When I say 'pass,' then pass your money to the person on your right."

After short intervals, the Facilitator says "Stop", and people stop passing. "What happened?"

After a group discussion, the process begins, and then, after a while, the facilitator says "Stop." This goes on for a few times until, finally, the Facilitator asks, "Shall we end this game?" Some people will have money, some will not.

Is it fair? How much money did you make?

There are several issues that will normally arise. Some people will hoard; others will not care. Holodynes take over. It is up to the Facilitator to identify the holodynes that are controlling the process.

Prosperity is a process, an ongoing act of giving. It does not matter to whom one gives or whether one ends up with money or not. The process of "passing" can be experienced from a particle mentality (how much do I have at this moment in time), a wave dynamic (it is an endless wave of receiving and giving) or a Holodynamic process (it is a game we have chosen to play). Prosperity is one whole dynamic.

Manifesting

The objective of the team is to *manifest*. Goals are to be met; prime conditions are to be set for life; and the team moves on to other aspects of choosing and completing its mission. You get results. If you don't get results, you go back and assess what is really wanted, checking in with your Full Potential Self. Do a reassessment with your team members; readjust your goals and objectives; change your structure; check on the principles you have been following; and re-align with the field dynamics.

Exercise 21: Review and bench marks

Review with your team a specific objective that you would like to manifest. Using the potentializing process, identify the benchmarks that will indicate your success and project a time line. Using time management procedures, keep track of the rate of manifes-

tation. Make notes:

1. I WANT TO MANIFEST THE FOLLOWING:
2. MY TEAM CONSISTS OF THE FOLLOWING PLAYERS:
3. OUR TEAM STRATEGY AND STRUCTURES ARE AS FOLLOWS:
4. THE PRINCIPLES UPON WHICH WE HAVE AGREED ARE AS FOLLOWS:
5. OUR BENCHMARKS ARE:

_____

_____

_____

_____

_____

_____

_____

_____

_____

_____

_____

_____

CHAPTER FOUR

SYNERGISTICS

ynergy refers to that extra energy that comes from a successful synapse. In other words, the sum of the whole is greater than the sum of the parts. If a certain crystal (palladium for example) can be caused to resonate with a certain frequency, it will give out as much as 5,000 units of energy for every unit fed into it. This is called "free" energy. In reality all energy is "free." Still, we doubt that by putting our heads and hearts into a project, we can expect "free" energy. That, however, is exactly what happens.

You can see it all the time in sports, business and government. Team members who reach that state of being in harmony with one another and aligned with the potential of their stated mission always experience synergism. They personally receive "free" energy, get "pumped up" and become "unstoppable." When this happens, the entire audience jumps to its feet and cheers.

The energy is there. It is available. It is just waiting to be used. You can use it. All you have to do is learn to "tap" the field.

TAPPING THE FIELD

Tapping the field means aligning with the harmonics that release the energy for your use. To tap the field is easy if you follow the potentializing process. The *field* is conscious. It is an information flow. Within the information flow are the processes by which information takes on form. One of the forms of information is energy. You can tap the field and tune in to the energy by understanding the motion that gives form to everything.

The information is always in motion. It follows certain patterns and these patterns give form to everything in our universe. These forms are the holodynes of our past, present and future. They exist within our microtubules and they govern the way we sense this world. They govern our fine-grained and gross-grained screens that cover our senses. The holodynes only allow us certain amounts of energy, only certain views of reality and only certain ways to experience things until we choose to take control.

Your source and your course are determined by your Full Potential Self. You can choose to take control and ask for guidance from your Full Potential Self. Once "on course", you will find yourself able to distinguish with much more accuracy. You can, for example, sense what holodynes are in control. You can access them and potentialize them. You can also enter the past and potentialize it through "reliving". You can potentialize the future by "preliving".

"RELIVES" – TEAMS FROM THE PAST

The key to unlocking the knowledge of the past and transforming its fields is to "relive" it. Take new information into it. Recognize you are not separated from the past. It runs now. Furthermore, the relationships you have with people in the past are all present and working now. You can use these relationships in the present. Just team up with them and potentialize your team in the present.

"PRELIVES" – TEAMS FROM THE FUTURE

The same is true of the relationships you have in the future. Most people think the future will happen sometime "in" the future, as though time were linear. Only a linear mind thinks time is linear. A Holodynamic mind understands that time is everywhere, "everywhen", and everyone. Once you "step out" of linear time, you are *present* whenever and wherever your Full Potential Self wants you to be present. Your ability to access the future allows you to bring the team in from the future and create the future in the now.

Exercise 22: The following five exercises are designed to prepare your team to conduct "relives" and "prelives" concerning the field dynamics of your team.

1. *Create a collage of your project.*
2. *Outline your family tree and identify the patterns passed on regarding teamwork.*
3. *Create a Round Table representative for each stage of development (see the Bird's-Eye View Chart) regarding your project.*
4. *Have each person "relive" their past lives, looking through the eyes of their Full Potential Self and shifting their own field dynamics so they are fully aligned with the Full Potential of the Being of Systems Synergy (BOSS) of their project.*
5. *Have each person "prelive" the future and bring the potential of the BOSS into the now.*

This process will tap into the field and allow the necessary energy to be successful in meeting your team goals. It is a complex process so it will require micro-management.

MICROMANAGEMENT

One key to success is micromanagement. Information transforms from the micro to the macro. If the small units work, the larger units work. If the small units don't work, the larger one won't either. Even if the larger system works, it does not assure you that the smaller one is working until you hit upon needing the smaller unit. Parts of the whole can work but parts can be dysfunctional. So, starting with holodynes, making sure your internal micro-world works assures you that your personality and relationships work. When everyone has their act together and their relationships are working, the entire team can be effective. Getting the entire system into harmony is what can happen during a "relive" and "prelive" process.

It takes courage to travel into your inner world, explore your past and transform those holodynes, shift the field and bring the potential future into the now. Even if it solves some of the most complex problems we have, it still requires (and deserves) some strategic planning. Effective teamwork and good business require effective strategic planning.

Strategic Planning

Strategic planning refers to a mapping process that takes in the whole dynamic of any set of circumstances and potentializes it. Individuals, teams, corporations and systems can benefit from strategic planning. Tools for strategic planning include such things as: systems analysis, daily planning, a bird's-eye view and prosperity consciousness.

Systems Analysis

Every system is a living thing. It has a formal and an informal, as well as a rational and an emotional aspect to its nature. It has structure and function, rules and regulations, metaphors and mechanisms. In the field dynamics, it is a living, growing, emerging potential, unfolding its information complexities, much like molten steel hardening to the mold of the mind of its participants.

The formal/rational/structural/rules/regulations/mechanisms of the system are usually outlined in the articles of incorporation, bylaws, mission statement, policies and procedures manual, business plan, benchmarks and budget allocations.

The informal/functional/metaphoric/inter-relationship dynamics of the system are rooted in how well people get along, in addition to their friendships, respect and concern for one another.

The formal and informal combine - like the left hand and the right hand, the left brain and the right brain, particle and wave - as part of the whole/living/conscious/causal system. Like everything else in the world, systems are conscious. They grow according to an implicate order and have their moments of life and death.

When conducting any analysis of any system, these three aspects (particle, wave and presence) are vital to understanding how it works and what it needs to unfold its highest and best potential. Management surveys often communicate more information to the workers within a system than do management policy declarations. Surveys give detailed summaries of question - and - answer data sheets. Most of the time, management briefly peruses these summaries, but company policy is seldom related to the facts that have been so painstakingly gathered. Usually, decisions are made based upon a completely different and often completely independent process.

Exercise 23: Discuss with your team the process that determines management of a system. Cluster some of the dynamics involved in this process. Discuss these with your team.

Daily Planning

Kirk Rector and I wrote a "Quick Start" booklet on how to organize a Potentializer Planner. The idea was to help people organize their time so they could better manage "taking the course." We had it translated into Russian and printed thousands of copies. When we flew into Moscow, the books were part of our luggage. However, when we went to pick up the books, an unknown party had already signed them out. We never recovered the books. The theft was not part of our conscious plan.

Our English edition met with a similar fate. We did all the work of organizing in detail but, when it came to the printing, the printer was six months into the year by the time the Personal Potentializer Planner was ready. It had 47 mistakes, including the pages being punched too far in so you could not turn the pages. It was not a marketable product. I had often wondered why we did not succeed in this aspect of the business.

Several years later, I attended a speech by Margaret Wheatley, author of "The New Science of Management." Margaret has done a masterful job of applying quantum thinking to the world of management, and I was excited to hear her. She did not disappoint me. Her work was outstanding. During the speech, one of the attendees asked what she thought of Steven Covey's work on management training. Margaret's reply struck right to the core of the issue. She said, "Planning does not work."

Planning does not work when the team is not coherent. When the work itself is linear, not integrated with the whole dynamic, the work cannot be potentialized. Too many people think they can think it through, plan their work and then work their plan.

Working doesn't work either. What works is *presence.*

Team members must first accept *the state of being the mission*, wherein each participant accepts ownership of the project. Ownership is an alliance between you and your Full Potential Self. It is a deep harmonic that attests to the course you are to take. It is a relationship between yourself first, down among your holodynes. Your Round Table guides must all agree to the mission. It is also a coalition among every participant in the field. It is a living, dynamic flow of energy and information. A knowing, loving, intensity that cannot be stopped.

I lost part of that with regard to the planners. I knew they were just tools, but I thought planning worked. I worked out a plan with Kirk; it was a good plan, but neither of us really took ownership of the project. Our personal dynamics were not connected to the work.

Plans and work itself are the byproducts of a state of being. Without that state of Being One with everyone involved, you can paper your walls with plans and they still won't work. So the first step is to obtain and maintain that state of being in "ownership" of the project. You *are* the project; you *are* the mission; and you *are* the *system*; then the plan will work. The plan will work because the state of being creates the synergy of success.

Exercise 24: How does each individual become the Main Mission of the system?

Discuss and outline your team's suggestions. Then have a team representative report to the larger group. The report can be interesting in itself. One way to give such a report is to have each team summarize in one or two words each main point on a white sheet of paper with a large colored pen. These sheets can be pasted on the board at the front of the conference room. You can then ask the group how each sheet relates to each of the others. The instructor uses the Mind Model to show the relationship among the words and demonstrates how the exercise itself is a living system.

Use a Bird's-Eye View

Leadership is about stewardship. An effective leader is a steward, a caretaker of a field of responsibility. A "Bird's-Eye View" refers to that epicenter from which a steward can see the entire stewardship. Like a bird, flying over a home, farm, factory or network of information, the bird can see the whole picture. A steward is not locked into an event horizon that is smaller than the stewardship.

Suppose, for example, you are starting a new business. Most people do not have a way to rise above their daily struggles such as meeting demands and schedules, getting the product out on time and under budget, adhering to principles and meeting the demands of the market. They may find themselves barely able to "crawl" from Point A to Point B, let alone "fly" above the dynamics like a bird. But taking a Bird's-Eye View is exactly doing just that. They must rise above their crisis-management habits, inexperience and limiting holodynes and give themselves permission to shift to an expanded view.

Any stewardship has an order of development. It has a management process and leadership potential. In the **Bird's-Eye View Chart,** you will find that each of the dimensions of the chart reflects the stewardship domains of a normal business. I have used the six stages of development of the Implicate Order as outlined in the Mind Model to create this chart. Start at the bottom of the chart (the foundation) in the left hand corner and go up vertically. You will see sample questions that must be answered for each stewardship domain as the system moves from its physical beginnings to developing its identity. The chart then outlines how to set up communication and commitments, contracting for other systems support, evaluation and quality control and marketplace integration.

Exercise 25: In addition to answering these questions for each stewardship domain of a normal business as shown in the chart, also try answering these questions for your project as a whole, using the project and its Being of Systems Synergy as the entity answering. Does this make a difference in how you see your project as part of a context? As

part of your community, your island, your culture, your planet?

From a "Bird's-Eye view," the project looks like a Round Table. You stand at the center of your information system. Your information resonates outward to embed itself into other systems. These information systems, when you hold their field, begin to manifest what the collective team wants. You "launch" the project. A new information system begins to manifest. In most business manuals, this dynamic flowing multidimensional field of information would look like this:

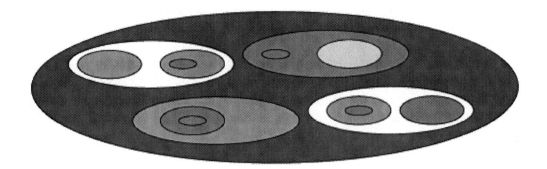

There is no need for pyramids of power in this model. All people stand on an equal footing, all at the same level. Each leader has different responsibilities; each must coordinate with those responsible for their entire stewardship; each "resides within" a wider stewardship; and information flows within and among each system according to unfolding potential.

Exercise 26: Discuss with your team the implications and applications of this model.

One of the guiding principles of team performance is that everyone's contribution is potentially a contribution and must be acceptable to the team. If we were part of an orchestra, the violin player cannot stand in judgment of the drummer. Both play in their own way but both must play.

Exercise 27: Point A to B

In this exercise the Presenter has the chairs in football formation, facing each other in two curves. Those on one side are designated "team A" those on the other side "team B."

This can be a lot of fun. The Presenter may call upon participants to compete with each other in clapping to see which team goes first. The entire class becomes involved and the winning team has to get from Point A to Point B in an entirely unique way. "If anyone does it the same as anyone else, they must come back to Point A and do it over in a unique way."

The observing team (referees), make sure it is done "right." Of course, there is no right or wrong way to get from Point A to Point B. It is just a game we make up and that is one of the points to be made in this exercise. Another point is that life, or the path we choose in life, can be followed in original and creative ways. The class will offer other lessons (not judging, there is no way to do it the same, etc.).

Exercise 28: Project Launch

Participants organize a specific project. It is recommended you make this project re-lated to the program of Holodynamics because everyone has it as a common reference. Other projects can be organized later.

Using the potentializing process, identify a project each team member has a common interest in seeing potentialized. Using the Bird's-Eye View of Business Development Dynamics Chart, each step of the project is planned out. Team Leaders are chosen and their plan is presented to the group as a whole. Feedback is given and, if necessary, the Team readjusts its plan.

Team members who are skilled at each specific horizontal dynamic, i.e., management, administration, human resources, research and development, operations, financing or marketing and public relations, offer services. Legal representatives are recommended; budgets are set; business plans complete; financing arranged; and the entire project is launched.

Another "Holodynamic" view of a business, project or organization is that it can be thought of as a living system, potentializing within other living systems. Jill Peters presents such a model in her article in the Appendix, "Sustainable Enterprise Development." This model places financial, social and environmental sustainability at the core of strategic planning, govern-ance, research and development, management practices, operations and relationships with stakeholders (which in Jill's model include future generations and the natural world). In this arti-cle, she discusses four critical stages in the evolution of a sustainable enterprise strategy, some involving environmental and socio-ethical sustainability practices, how to set up and measure core sustainability issues using a new "triple bottom line" and the return on a "triple bottom line" investment. You may want to review this article as you plan your project.

Whatever project or business model you use, it does not matter how big or small, how personal or international the project. What matters is that it meets the criteria for unfolding po-tential according to what really works. What really works is pretty much outlined in the Holody-namics program. Personal presence, responsibility, adherence to principles and contribution to life and establishing your own prime condition or the prime condition of others are some of the guiding principles. These will be discussed more in the next Intensive on principle - based dy-namics.

Exercise 29: Team Presenting

Organize into teams with the purpose in mind of presenting some aspect of Holodynamics. In some areas of the world, teams members are made of different people from different skills. One may be experienced at teaching. Another may be more familiar with the sciences, while another may be more interested in therapy or group dynamics. As a team, the effectiveness of the group increases.

Plan to meet together, develop a plan, potentialize your teaching and find a way to create its reality in society. Plan; also, to correlate with the rest of the Holodynamic Community so we can support you in your endeavors, get you the materials, supervise your work and participate in your project if you so desire. When you are ready, you may want to apply for certification as a Presenter.

Use the processes taught in this course to create your team.

MY TEAM PRESENTING MEMBERS ARE:

OUR PRIMARY TEAM MISSION IS:

OUR IDENTITY SHALL BE KNOWN AS:

OUR PLAN IS:

OUR CONNECTION TO THE HOLODYNAMIC PROGRAM SHALL BE:

WE WILL NEED THE FOLLOWING ASSISTANCE FROM THE FOLLOWING PEOPLE:

WE COMMIT TO THE FOLLOWING PRINCIPLES:

WE PLAN TO EXTEND OUR EFFORTS IN THE FOLLOWING MANNER:

CHAPTER FIVE

PROSPERITY CONSIOUSNESS

THERE ARE A WIDE VARIETY OF POSSIBILITIES AVAILABLE WHEN USING A HOLODY-NAMIC APPROACH. In reality, almost any path is in a state of continual self-improvement. Financial responsibility and prosperity consciousness are no exceptions. The following are examples:

Business Courses in Holodynamics

Perhaps the most electrifying breakthrough in the modern business world is the realization that there is no absolute reality out there waiting to be discovered. We all live, breathe and have our being in an interactive, intelligent, holographic universe that responds to our presence. Understanding the dynamic nature of reality provides the most accurate predictors available. This new information gives every business a distinct advantage. In order to share this leading edge, we have designed the following courses that we present in this manual:

1. Empowering Potential
2. Success Circles

When we meet with people in leadership situations, we bring to the table certain tools that work to help participants unfold their personal and organizational potential. We recognize the genius in each individual and the potential we share in this age of new sciences and new information networks. We create the course together. The facilitators will model within each group an intimate, active creative process that applies the new sciences personally and helps integrate their practical application into the world of organizational empowerment. It is a deeply personal experience - one participants enjoy and that invites a long-term relationship between our team and your company.

Organizations have the opportunity to —

- Empower the potential in every facet of corporate culture;
- Empower the potential of every individual in the company;
- Gain access to new information world-wide;
- Acquire high tech tools to leverage their resources;
- Capitalize on outside, independent contractors;
- Manage rapid growth with skill and cooperative teamwork;
- Manage daily operations with new, more complete accuracy; and
- Use the new sciences to better predict and prepare for the future.

In the 21st century, organization and business is about personal, informed, empowered, living relationships between highly educated and universally conscious people.

New information networks bring to the fingertips of every team member the necessary communication devices, banking capabilities, information sources and contracting abilities to acquire, manufacture or service mobile networks, not just in your own neighborhood, but around the globe.

In order to meet the requirements of the new Information Age, every business must enter the 21st century prepared for the new ways of doing business. This means corporate structures must be more fluid and less rigid, more democratic and less autocratic, as well as more personal and less automatic. In a work environment that is responsive to personal and cultural tastes and provides more life - oriented space, employees are more self-motivated. In fact, they become more self-employed. Corporate jobs are more specialized. Information networks allow individual contracting of a wide range of adaptable, professional services at great savings to companies. Management must learn to respond to a more participatory universe.

People will be working more from their homes, servicing the company rather than having an office in a company building. Already, many companies, including some of the Fortune 500 companies, are downsizing. The interesting thing is that even though some large companies have downsized by 80 percent, they are still able to maintain their services to customers. Linked by advanced computers and tied in by contracted relationships, independent professionals are becoming more and more important to the overall success of a business. They are giving contractors an "edge" over businesses that require control over their employees. New leadership models are preparing for this inevitability.

The Information Age, with its mobilization of resources and its redistribution of wealth and power, is already under way. It is an age of remarkable opportunity for those willing to meet the challenges.

Effective businesses are now centering on people, their resources and their networks. More than ever, complex jobs are being accomplished by specialized people networks linked via high - technology information systems. The flexibility, skills, imagination, initiative, loyalty, dedication, creativity and stability of the people involved *are* the company. Without adequate contracted networks, a company cannot compete in the 21st century. If a company expects to run things in "the same old way," it cannot hope to reach its potential. The basic assumptions have all changed.

Empowering Potential

The Empowering Potential courses provide a team of consultants who conduct modules of participatory "Empowering" experiences within the company. Each module takes the team closer to the 21st century and prepares the company for a future that is already upon us. The Empowering Potential path suggests the following modules:

Module One: Personal Growth and Development

1. Exploring the potential within - the "geni - us,"

2. Success as a quantum state and a process,

3. Creating a more comprehensive personal reality,

4. Inner games people play and inner dialogues that run the show,

5. Taking responsibility for team participation,

6. Focusing on potential,

7. Empowering potential,

8. Building a personal money-management system,

9. Managing time,

10. Focusing on Holodynamic solutions,

In this first module, participants discover their own personal power and how they can make a difference to the corporate team. A company's investment in its people in their personal exploration, understanding, and growth - are the best investments a company can make in its own future.

Module Two: Building Highly Proficient Teams

11. Dynamics of communication,

12. Processes of team building,

13. Focusing on the potential of the team,

14. Creating a team path to success,

15. The games team members play,

16. Taking responsibility for team participation,

17. Empowering team potential,

18. The life of the team,

In this second module, participants learn cooperation and teamwork, plus the skills of how to operate within their fullest potential together, as part of a fluid and highly efficient team.

Module Three: Building a Corporate Culture

19. Participation from a Holodynamic perspective,

20. The flow of dynamics in a corporate culture,

21. Focusing on corporate potential,

22. Creating a corporate path to success,

23. Management by dynamic participation,

24. Empowering corporate potential,

25. The life of the company,

In the third module, participants concentrate upon company potential and how to team together to select priorities, form necessary relationships and accomplish their common vision.

Empowering Potential is an ongoing process within a corporate culture. It provides a path to follow to come to that state of being in which each person "becomes the team." They come to identify with the company as a living, dynamic field of excitement that provides personal satisfaction and collective accomplishment. Business is an ongoing, intimate, cultural experience.

By getting to know themselves, participants get to know each other, as well as trust and support one another in personal dynamic ways. They look at each other as friends, with families, strengths and the usual run of weaknesses. They become part of the corporate community of real people with personal dreams and hopes. They share their inner selves and their real outer world.

Creating a corporate culture that encourages a continual developmental path for its team is good business. It is good business in any age but, in this age, it is essential to future success.

Empowering Potential provides —

- Increased self-awareness and self-esteem;
- Increased responsibility and self-initiated behavior;
- Increased creativity and commitment to corporate objectives;
- Decreased time away from the job;

- Decreased dependency on outside help;
- Decreased complaints and discontent;
- Increased depth of understanding about the new sciences and their applications to organizations;
- How to use the new sciences to create new views; and
- How to use the new views to empower personal and corporate potential.

Empowering Potential helps create a corporate culture that provides —

- A common corporate language about the dynamics of success;
- A process by which conflict is easily and effectively transformed;
- A culture opportunity beyond greed, self-serving, critical analysis, pyramids of power and all the old mechanistic thinking;
- A new language founded on solid principles of the new sciences and proven effective in the new business world; and
- A way of thinking about personal and corporate dynamics that is success and action - oriented, individually initiated and collectively accepted.

Empowering Potential offers an environment in which each person can reach into the reservoir of their own potential and find new ways to unfold that potential in the working world.

From Vision to Reality

There are specific procedures that move from dreams and visions to reality. Here are some examples:

1. FOCUS: Focus requires you to be clear and specific about what you want. The universe requires a clear picture, as free from contamination and contradictions as possible, in order to mobilize the field support necessary to give form to what you want.

2. PERSONALIZATION: Dreams are reflections of your potential. You must align your conscious desire with the harmonics of your Full Potential Self in order to manifest your real potential.

3. RECRUITMENT: You must find those of like mind, who have also aligned with what is wanted, and recruit them into an intimate working relationship in which all are agreed and committed to manifesting what is wanted.

4. SYNERGISM: Team building, assignment of responsibilities, decisions to act, carrying out of each responsibility and quality performance create extra energy or synergy among team members. This extra energy produces extraordinary results and births the system that carries on the work of manifesting what is wanted.

5. PRINCIPLE-DRIVE PROCESSES: Any organization that is principle-driven will create extraordinary results. Principles form the guiding essence by which systems grow.

6. INTEGRATION: From micro to macro, participants within a system "become" the system. They represent the collective mentality that unfolds the deep hidden potential of the living system.

7. EXTENSION: The life and growth of any potential depends upon its extension into the world of reality. Get real. Get going. Be your dream. Be the system that manifests your dream.

Each of the above are words we have wrapped around parts of a living process by which dreams come true. This living process is as much a science as it is an art, and as much a part of life as it is a mental exercise. Materializing dreams requires involving the whole dynamic.

Management and the 21st Century

Management and the 21st Century is an intensive course, usually conducted as a 10 - day retreat designed to create dynamic leadership teams for the next century. The course is held at a luxurious setting (as on the Big Island of Hawaii, within sight of dolphins, whales and beautiful reefs, and where island activities such as snorkeling, scuba diving, and golf on world acclaimed courses are available). The accommodations provide an ideal setting for in-depth, leadership training.

The course is usually held twice per year. Applicants must hold management positions and be pre-approved before registration. The number of participants is never more than 20 or fewer than 10. The course is designed specifically for each individual participant.

Exercise 30: What would you and your team like to experience, see taught, or teach in such a course? Outline and discuss with your team.

_____

_____

_____

_____

_____

_____

CIRCLES OF SUCCESS

There are seven Circles of Success programs. Each has a series of courses sponsored by the International Academy of Holodynamics. Below is a detailed Teacher's Outline of a three-day course on "Circles of Success." The Academy has a Power Point presentation (samples are included) that is available to certified teachers.

Exercise: Team up with those who want to teach courses. Make notes in the margins and discuss your objectives and teaching plan with your team.

INSTRUCTION OUTLINE: CIRCLE ONE

Day 1 - Holodynamics: "the whole dynamic"

Start time: 9:00 a.m.: Registration and Introduction

9:30 a.m.: The New Paradigm: Cosmology & Physics (foundation paradigm determines social/cultural belief systems)

A brief review of the history of consciousness: Greeks – middle Ages – Copernicus – Galileo – Newton – Einstein – new sciences – quantum physics – holographics – the science of consciousness, etc.

Holodynamics – Newest Paradigms: Quantum Physics/Cosmology/Developmental Psychology

- *Holodynamics focuses on the "full potential" in every situation.*
- *Holodynamics expands your senses and abilities!*
- *Holodynamics helps you get what you really want!*

Wall Charts

Mission of Holodynamics: (a series of posters)
Continually unfolding the Full Potential through successfully applying the principles and processes of Holodynamics worldwide.

Principles: (the Six Stages of Development Chart)
Physical Vitality – Personal Creativity – Interpersonal Intimacy
Social Synergy – Principled Integrity – Universal Oneness

Circles: All Circles are One Circle (chart)
Physical world - survival
Personal world – self-interest and personal development
Relationships – getting along with others

Professional world – team interest
Environment – planetary interest

ALL CIRCLES ARE ONE CIRCLE

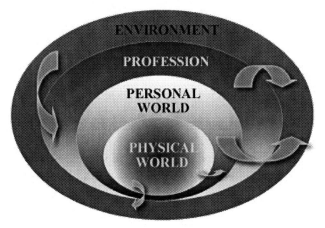

Information Organizes from Micro (smallness) to Macro (bigness):

ANY CIRCLE CAN BE POTENTIALIZED

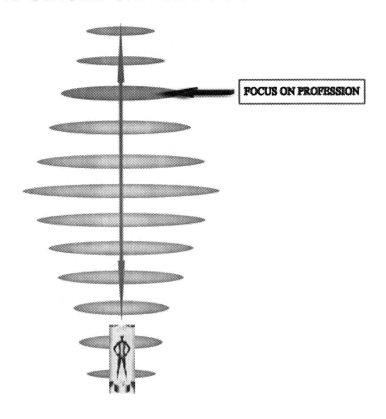

FOCUS ON PROFESSION

Seven Processes: (taught in this course)

Place of Peace –
Full Potential Self –
Field of Love –
Tracking holodynes
Round Table –
Potentializing –
Follow through (Holons).

Circle One: Training Goals:
~ **Provide principles and processes for unfolding your Full Potential!**
~ **Help you get what you really want!**
~ **Teach you initial processes of Holodynamics for daily use.**
~ **Give you immediate success so you can go on to Circle II.**

Rules of this course:
1. **Be on Time**
2. **Take Notes**
3. **Participate Fully! Learn the processes!**
4. **Everything that happens is part of seminar! (Before, during and after.)**
5. **Become Conscious of Your Choices! ("My page" in back of notes)**

10:45 a.m. Exercise 1: Using your Senses: (25 minutes)

External (ESP): seeing, hearing, smelling, tasting, feeling, subtle energy senses.
Internal (ISP): Internal seeing, hearing, smelling, tasting, feeling, subtle senses.

Pick Your Partner
Partners pick another couple and form Groups of Four.

11:10 a.m. Exercise 2: "What do I want from this seminar!" (30 minutes)

Individual work / Discuss with Partner / Group of Four
Reports – Put on wall

11:40 a.m. Recognize & Discuss "Field of Love"   Love = Recognition/Acceptance (10 minutes)

11:50 a.m. Exercise 3: "I accept you and support you in all that you do." (10 minutes)

Noon Break (15 minutes)

12:15 a.m. Instruction: Double - Slit Experiment (30 minutes)

Albert Einstein, Niels Bohr, Werner Hiesenburg, Erwin Schrödinger and John von Neumann; (Big Charts or Power Point Presentation)

1. Wave / Particle Nature of Universe
2. Wave – All Possible Positions – "In Potential" – "Many Worlds"
3. Particle = "Collapse" of Wave – "Measured" in 3D + Time
4. Particle: "aware" of all possibilities!
5. Heisenberg's Uncertainty Principle – "Free Choice" of the Quantum
6. Wave and Particle manifest "the Field" – 4 "Known" Fields – Unified Field – What is Consciousness? – What is choice?
7. Hyperspace: the demonstration of communication between photons that were traveling away from each other.

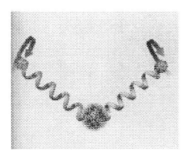

> Hyperspace: The EPR experiment demonstrated that communication between two bonded photons of light was possible even when they were traveling at the speed of light away from each other.

12:45 a.m. Discussion: How does this "Experiment" apply to my life? (15 minutes)

1:00 p.m. Instruction: Holographic Metaphor (45 minutes)

Example: Pass around a Hologram (5 minutes)

Holographic Plate–Subject–Laser–Hologram (Big Chart or Power Point Presentation)

1. Wave Unmanifest and Particle Manifest
2. Wave "many worlds" and Particle "one world"
3. Particle: "in the Mind of Beholder"
4. Wave: whole is known by Every Part!
5. Mind is Holographic
6. Universe is Holographic

1:45 p.m. Discussion: "How does Holographic metaphor apply to my life?" (15 minutes)

CIRCLES OF SUCCESS
CAN BE ACCOMPLISHED BY

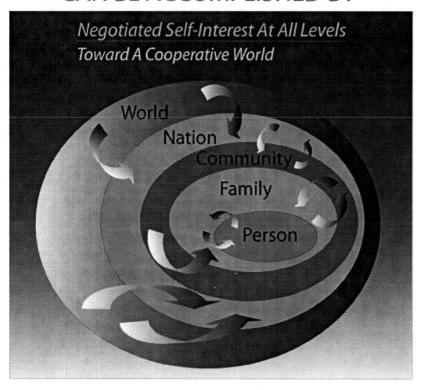

Negotiated Self-Interest At All Levels
Toward A Cooperative World

World
Nation
Community
Family
Person

In a quantum computer, one new byte of information resets the entire computer.

In Nature, self-interest can be presented in such a way that the entire biosphere resets itself.

Among humans…. (?)

2:00 p.m. Lunch–Eat and Exercise: "Trust Walk" (1 hour)

3:00 p.m. Discuss "Trust Walk" What happened? What did you learn? (30 minutes)

Individual makes notes/share in groups: Group Reports
(New awareness/focus/field of love with partner/new language/leaving comfort zone)

3:30p.m. Instruction: Qualities of a holodyne (30 minutes)

Including Exercises:
Play with "holodynes"–lemon, mother, first day of school, first kiss
Emphasis on "Focus"

Aspects of holodynes

1. "Holographic Thought Form"–Pribram/Woolf
2. Manifest in mind: color, shape, feel, smell, taste, subtle energies (all "inner senses "ISP")
3. Causal Potency"–ability to "cause" your actions Sperry/Penrose/Hammeroff
4. On the "edge" of 3D + Time - Many dimensions (at least 10)!

5. ("Holodynamic plane"/"quantum potential field")
6. How We Get holodynes:
7. Genetics
8. Mind Camera
9. Imagination
10. Parallel Worlds
11. Holodynes Organize into "Systems"
12. Holodynes "Play Games"
13. Holodynes never "die," they just go to another dimension!

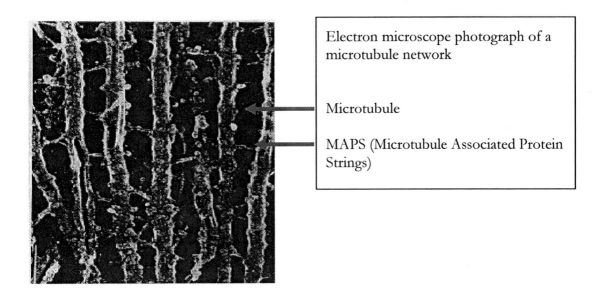

Electron microscope photograph of a microtubule network

Microtubule

MAPS (Microtubule Associated Protein Strings)

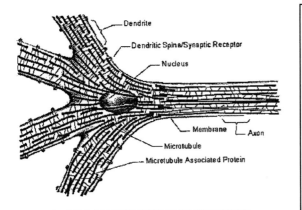

A NEURON WITH IT'S MICROTUBULES

HOLODYNES ARE
HOLOGRAPHIC IMAGES

HOLODYNES ARE STORED WITHIN THE WATER MEDIA OF THE MICRO-TUBULES

One of the central mechanisms of consciousness are the microtubules. Holodynes are formed in the microtubules. Microtubules make up the walls of every living cell. When the microtubules are anesthetized, consciousness stops.

The good news is that we can transform our holodynes.

Holodynes control our corporate environment.

4:00 p.m. Exercise: Place of Peace (20 minutes)

Individual Description–Draw–Sharing with Partner

This is my Place of Peace. I can go there whenever the job gets too hectic or chaos seems to be taking over.

No one can draw me into their chaos when I am centered in my Place of Peace.

From this state of being, I can take charge of my life.

4:20 p.m. Discuss Qualities and Uses of "Place of Peace" (10 minutes)

(archetypal symbols/altered state of consciousness/daily uses/instant access)

4:30 p.m. Exercise: Full Potential Self (20 minutes)

One of the basic findings of quantum physics is that every set of circumstances is driven by potential. Everything we consider to be "real" is made of information coming from a quantum field of potential. Everything is potential until it is given form. Every atom is made of spinners of information.

Every person has a Full Potential Self.

4:50 p.m. Discuss Qualities and Uses of "Full Potential Self" (10 minutes)

(access to "higher self" wisdom–power, tool for your intuition)

~ Home Assignment: Draw Place of Peace/Full Potential Self~

5:00 p.m. Break (15 minutes)

5:15 p.m. Instruction: "holodynes Form Systems and Play Games!" (20 minutes)

Basic Game Theory

1. Playing field (boundaries/time/space)
2. Players (separation & polarization–"them - us"/official/unofficial/spectators)
3. Goal (win - lose/win - win/lose - lose/of the game, of the individual players)
4. Rules (explicit/implicit)
5. Rule Keepers (formal/informal)
6. Strategy and Tactics (before/during/after)
7. What is "At Risk?"–"Jeopardy"
8. Mental States (holodynes of the game)
9. Game Level–inner game–manifest game–meta game

What games do you notice around you?
Physical? Personal? Interpersonal? Social? Principled? Universal?

Discuss: "money game!"

Discuss: life - death/young - old/male - female/and other games.

What choices are you making during these games?
What games do you want to play?
What games do you want to change, transform, or leave?

What "games" do you see in this picture?

Do the "games" change once you see the whole picture?

The mind is like a camera: "What you focus on is what you get."

5:35 p.m. Exercise: "What games do I (my holodynes) play?" (15 minutes)

(10 minute) inside the group, make list! (5 - Minutes) then brief group reports.
Physical? Personal? Interpersonal? Social? Principled? Universal?

Assignment: Between now and tomorrow–notice what games you and others play.

What choices are you making during these games?
What games do you want to play?
What games do you want to change, transform, or leave?

5:50 p.m. Final Assignment: Day Close/Day Start - Short Version (5 minutes)

Tonight and tomorrow morning, practice the following:

- Go to your Place of Peace
- Call upon your Full Potential Self
- Have a conversation–Ask questions–Receive messages–Give assignments
- Take Notes!
- Be ready to report tomorrow

5:55 p.m. Closing–Large Group Field of Love (5 minutes)

"I accept you, and support you in all that you do!"

6:00 p.m. Night Assignments

1. **Draw Place of Peace/Full Potential Self**
2. **Notice the "games" holodynes are playing–yours and others! Notice what "choices" you are making during the games!**
3. **Invite at least 2 friends or family to the "Graduation Party"**
4. **Day Close/Day Start Process**

Day 2: Holodynes & Tracking

10:00 a.m. Reports: "What happened after 6:00pm last night, until now!" (30 minutes)

Groups meet and discuss:

Drawings of Place of Peace–Full Potential Self
Day 1 Close/Day 2 Start
"Games" I play; I want to play; I don't want to play.

Reports/Question and Answers

Some people think of their job as having a tiger by the tail.

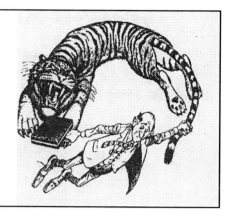

10:30 a.m. Elements of the Psyche–A System of holodynes (30 minutes)

The Chooser/The Persona/The Conscious/The Unconscious
"Archetypes"/The Shadow/Anima & Animus/"Potential"

When your job feels like a pit-bull experience, what can you possibly do?

Projections–"Negative"

What makes me angry? Spiteful? Jealous? Sad? Pessimistic?
Negative patterns I repeat
Accidents

Projections–"Positive"

What do I "sense" about my "potential? What do I dream about?
What goals?
Heroes? Mentors? What do I really want?

Full Potential Self

11:00 a.m. Exercise: What do I project? (30 minutes)

> *"Negative"*
> *"Positive"*
> Reports/Put on Wall
> **When I "project, what choices do I make?—Conscious/Unconscious?**

11:30 a.m. Break: (15 minutes)

11:45 a.m. Game: Point A to Point B: Sculpturing holodynes (30 minutes)

Exercise: Empowering Full Potential Self—Group of Four (30 minutes)

> Group of four in a circle
> One person at a time stands—"in his or her Full Potential!"
> Group expresses qualities they sense about his Full Potential Self.
> Partner writes comments in person's notebook.

12:45 p.m. Instruction: Mind Model I (1 hour)

> Family Belief System/Social Belief System/Right & Left Brain/Six Levels/Interest Wave
> *Six Level Chart*
> Map of your holodynes—Natural Development—Updraft/Downdraft Dynamics
> *Conscious Choosing = Commitment to yourself!*

Group Assignments: Tomorrow - Role Plays of Physical & Personal Level

1:45 p.m. Reports and Discussion (30 minutes)

> What happened? What did you feel? What did you want?
> What did you learn? Can you recognize the holodynes?
> Access holodynes: feeling?–body?–color?–shape?–what is it doing?–what does it want?

2:00 p.m. Lunch (1 hour)

3:00-3:30 p.m. Demonstration: Tracking (30 minutes)

Instruction: How to Track–Circle Model–18 Tracking Steps

3:30 p.m. Break (15 minutes)

3:45 p.m. Instruction: Tracking Session Rules (5 minutes)

1. During the Session–We Focus! We Track!
   (We don't just "talk about" tracking; we don't "philosophize;" we don't escape! We track. If we can't track, we track what's keeping us from tracking!)
2. We stay in the room during the session. Don't wander out.
3. If we finish, we discuss the tracking–then switch partners.

We prepare to share our experience with the larger group.

5:30 p.m. Break (10 minutes)–*Distribute Tracking Guide*

5:40 p.m. Exercise: First Tracking Session (50 minutes)

> Track holodyne from "My Page"–Partner Tracking

6:30 p.m. Reports–Question and Answers (20 minutes)

- Clusters
- Using a guide
  Assignment: Tonight– **Track one other person.**
  Track yourself–Using Tracking Guide

6:50 p.m. Closing Exercise: "Vision of What I Really Want!" (10 minutes)

> Meditation–Place of Peace–Full Potential
> What in your life do you feel as a new potential?
> What do I really want! Visualize all Six Levels
> Symbol–(Start to Draw–Finish Symbol Tonight–Place on the wall tomorrow.

Assignment:

>   Draw "symbol" for what you really want!
>   Collage of pictures from magazines–"*what I want*" visualization tool

7:00 p.m. Close: Night assignment

1.   Verify at least two people who will attend "graduation party" 4:45p.m. on the evening of the last day of this course.
2.   Draw "symbol" for what you really want!
3.   Collage of pictures from magazines–"*what I want*" visualization tool
4.   Track one other person
5.   Track yourself
6.   Day 2 Close/ Day 3 Start Process

Day 3–Holodyne Party!

10:00 a.m. Reports: "What happened (after 6:00pm until now!) (20 minutes)

>   Groups–share "symbol" and pictures on the wall.
>   What happened: tracking one other person/tracking yourself?
>   Day 2 Close/Day 3 Start?

10:20 a.m. Groups Report to Large Group (10 minutes)

10:30 a.m. Instruction "Morphogenetic Fields" (20 minutes)

>   Projection of Full Potential into 3D+ Time.

The Biology of Business

10:45 a.m. Review of the processes used in Nature for resolving conflicts of self interest.

Circles of Development

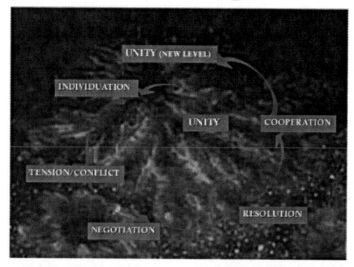

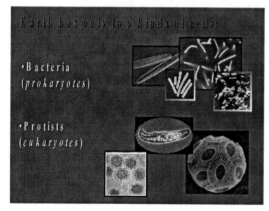

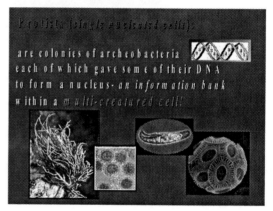

Ancient bacteria created complex multi-celled life forms (radiolarian designs, for example), veins of pure minerals, continental shelves, ocean chemistry and an atmosphere that contains 20percent oxygen. They also pioneered complex cities, city-states and even imperialistic forms of government. All life forms are in symbiotic relationship to one another.

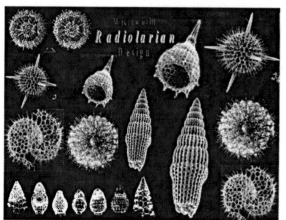

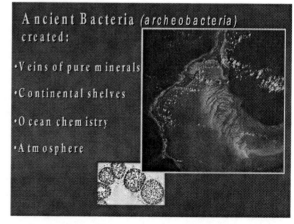

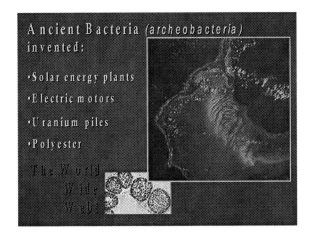

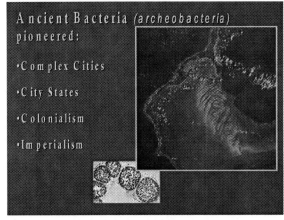

In biology, it is clear that every species is part of the harmonics of Nature. Everything symbiotically woven into the web of life. Earth is a magnificent matrix.

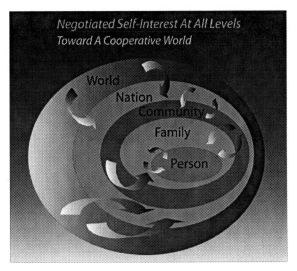

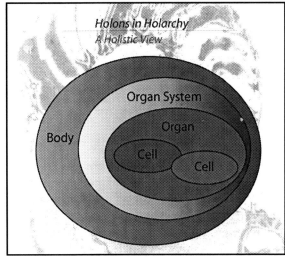

We are embedded within a great holarchy of information. At its most finite source, we emerge from the quantum potential field of hyperspace as spinners of information that give form to our DNA, organize our microtubules, form our cells, develop our neurons and provide us with conscious capacity. We are born, develop personality, create relationships, become part of a family system, join in social activities and organize into groups. Groups form associations, corporations, nations and international relationships develop. We are extending into the stars.

THE GREAT HOLARCHY

WE ARE EMBEDDED IN THE MIDDLE OF A GREAT HOLARCHY OF INFORMATION

Review: How does Nature conduct its business?

> How does Nature resolve conflicts?
> What can we learn from Nature?

11:30 a.m. Break (15 minutes)

11:45 a.m. Tracking Session II–"Physical" holodynes (1 hour)

12:45 p.m. Reports of Tracking–Question and Answer (15 minutes)

1:00 p.m. Early Lunch (1 hour)

2:00 p.m. Role Plays: Personal holodynes–(30 minutes)

> – Role Play

— Accessing the holodynes
— Discovering the "unmanifest" dynamic

2:30 p.m. Tracking Session III–Personal holodynes (45 minutes)

3:15 p.m. Reports of Tracking–Question and Answer (15 minutes)

Power of Tracking in your life!–How it expands your ability to choose!

3:30 p.m. Break (15 minutes)

3:45 Vision of Circles II–III–IV–V–VI - VII (15 minutes)

Wall Charts–(Hand out Training Schedule, 90 - Day Calendars)

Circle II – Personal And Interpersonal Dynamics – "Tracker" Certification

Circle III – Interpersonal and Family Dynamics – "Relive" and Group Field Shift

Circle IV – Social Systems Dynamics – "Presenter" Certification

Circle V – Principled Leadership Program – Teacher Certification

Circle VI – Universal Directorship Program – Mater Certification

Circle VII – Extension – Doctorate Certification

What is Tracker Certification? What is Certification in each Circle?

Requirements for Cycle II – Personal and Interpersonal Dynamics:

1. Follow your 90 - Day Plan for getting what you want…Track and Transform "obstacles" and "problems.
2. Empower your new holodynes!
3. Tracking Manual: Make notes of your Tracking.
4. Apply Day Start / Day Close – Keep notes in Tracking Book
5. Attend Weekly Holon Meetings – (get date and times). Bring new people!
6. Work with partner and group of four.
7. Enroll another person into Circle I:

   — Demonstrate your commitment
   — Deal with interpersonal relationships
   — For each additional person you enroll (after your first) you receive credit toward your next Circle.

Working with "Group of 4"

–   Share telephone numbers and schedules.
–   Commit to support and empower the Full Potential of each person.
–   Track each other – whenever obstacles or problems arise!

Special Discount for committing to Cycle II – TODAY:
Special credit when you enroll another person who pays. (Thus: If you enroll another person by Friday the effect is a certain percentage off the price!)

4:00 p.m. Prepare Cycle I Personal Commitments (20 minutes)

Goals and General Plan for the Next 90 Days! (Use 90 - Day Calendars)
Goals are "Commitments" to Yourself!
What Commitments are you making to unfold your potential?

–   List Commitments
–   Set Goals
–   Outline General Plan for next 90 days
–   Who will be attending Cycle II?

4:20 p.m. Meditation – about future – Unfolding Your Potential (10 minutes)

Circle–Closed Eyes!

Envision yourself going for what you really want…
…transforming your obstacles… … reaching your goals…
… Being, Doing, Having What You Really Want!

4:30 p.m. Friends Appear – OPEN EYES! (15 minutes)

Celebration!
Expressing Feelings and Commitments!

4:45 p.m. Graduation Ceremony (15 minutes)

Award Certificates for Cycle I
Further Expressing of Commitments and Feelings!

5:00–6:00 p.m. (…and beyond…)   PARTY !!

Singing / Music / Dancing / Social / FUN!

CIRCLES OF SUCCESS

THE CORPORATE CIRCLE

INTRODUCTION

Meeting the daily challenges on the job is vital to both our personal success and the success of the company. It is part of our organizational life together and deserves not only our focus but also our complete mastery. Toward this end, part of our job description becomes to create optimum cooperation, to encourage everyone's creativity and establish effectiveness within the entire system.

Professional ability is woven into the life fabric of the corporation. It is part of our company trust and is required within the integrity of the system. The degree that we can master our profession determines the success of our company. Because of this basic reality, we must now continue to focus on the "Corporate" Circle of Success and we will continue to focus until every member of the team is able to master the skills necessary to maintain success in this circle.

KEY ELEMENTS OF SUCCESS WITHIN THE CORPORAT CIRCLE:

How do we as career professionals within Circles of Success, master the "Corporate Circle" of Success? Here are a few examples of subjects we can explore that will help us achieve our fullest professional potential within the company.

1. THE MULTIPLE BOTTOM LINE

Every company has a "bottom line" - the fundamental element that measures success. In this company, we have a *multiple* bottom line. Each professional must understand and support the bottom line in order for the company to be successful.

A. PEOPLE:

People are the heart of the company. People include not just those within the company headquarters, but those who are customers, or potential customers, out in the field. People are "everything" to Circles of Success. Without customers, we would not exist. People come first. Everyone must master their people communication skills and learn to deal effectively with each other and with customers in the field.

B. SERVICE:

Our primary product is service. We serve the public. Every person in this company must develop and maintain a state of being that is service centered. This is what we do and we must all do it well, professionally, with skill.

C. PRODUCTS:

The Products of Circles of Success are the essence of our success. Our Products are the vehicle that forges the public image of who we are and what we do. Every person in this company must be not only familiar with each product, but must also have used the products and be able to stand for their quality and necessity.

WE sell the products. Our sales effort is not just some abstract or "out there" action. Sales is the primary, bottom line action of the people in this company. This includes everyone - the package - delivery personnel, secretaries, computer personnel, management, etc. - everyone.

D. PROFITS:

There is a primary relationship between assets and profits. In order for any company to be successful, this relationship between assets and profits. This relationship, once understood and supported by everyone in the company, helps produce a healthy profit and that means a healthy company.

The distribution of profit is directly related to the assets invested within the company. Assets include not only money invested in the manufacture of products or the management of the office, but also the hours of labor spent by each person, the quality of service, creativity contributions and team effort are also part of the assets of a company. When products are sold, each asset invested deserves a fair share of the revenues received.

E. INTEGRITY:

When a company is principle-driven and everyone is aligned, a special synergy occurs. This synergy produces extra - energy within a company that drives it forward to accomplish its mission. This internal integrity provides the necessary power to maintain the company through the challenges of doing business in a competitive world. This is why internal integrity is an essential part of any healthy business.

F. TRANSPARENCY:

The Information Age has created a new level of sophistication within corporations. It is now possible to have everyone within a company understand the operations of the company. Corporate life has become transparent. Everyone has become involved in the success of the company. No more "klepto-bureaucrats," secret deals, hidden profits, or unfair distributions. Everything and everyone is transparent.

G. QUALITY OF LIFE:

Everyone wants to live according to a chosen quality of life. We work in order to establish and maintain our own preferred quality of life. This includes our world of work. We each collaborate to create a corporate culture that reflects a sustainable, desirable, quality of life.

When our work environment is good, our life is better. Quality of life is essential to our work. Who is responsible for our quality of life at work? We are. It is up to us and no one else. We get to choose our quality of life on the job.

H. INTEGRATION:

Our corporate life cannot in reality, be separated. We are all connected - to other systems and to our personal and community life. It requires integration in order to survive. Each of us is responsible for maintaining the integrative network that sustains the corporation.

2. OUR MISSION

The Mission Statement of Circles of Success is to assist in unfolding the potential of each participant.

Each corporate team member should know this statement and follow it. This applies to internal and external dynamics. We have a multiple bottom line that includes everything from our individual holodynes to our global impact. We include people, the business and the community. Unfolding potential is our "guiding star" and keeps us aligned with what we are teamed-up to accomplish. Our corporate logo, products and processes reflect our mission. Our actions are a testament as to its validity.

3. KEEPING ON TRACK

In order to help us attain professional success, the company is conducting the Circles of Success meetings. We are experiencing what is called "rapid growth" and in order to stay "on track" the Friday training session is designed to help us all achieve increased corporate success and stay on track.

4. TRAINING OTHERS

The Academy has prepared a series of course and presentations on the enfolded dimensions of business. I want to give you an idea of the content of these courses and so below, I have outlined the topics of one of the presentations. Experienced leaders who are teachers in the corporate world give these presentations. What follows is a brief outline of the content of one of these presentations.

This particular presentation takes place in an open discussion format of approximately 45 minutes for each session. Each session develops into the next. Only the titles of the subjects are presented in this text since the pictures and the information are proprietary to the Academy.

SESSION ONE: THE ENFOLDED DIMENSIONS OF BUSINESS

NEGOTIATED SELF-INTEREST AND PROFESSIONAL COHERENCE: NEGO-

TIATED SELF-INTEREST AND A HEALTHY STATE OF BEING; TAPPING THE SOURCE OF YOUR PROFESSIONAL POTENTIAL; PROFESSIONAL FOCUS

ENFOLDED DIMENSIONS: EXPANDING YOUR FOCUS; THE HOLOGRAPHIC DIMENSION AND THE POWER TO CAUSE; CREATIVE IMAGINATION; FOCUS ON REALITY: ALL OF REALITY. THE "GENI - IN - US"; THE SYMBIOTIC TEAM.

The assumption of this session is that life has been around a lot longer than humans and we can learn a lot from what has gone on before we came along. After all, we want to be successful and there is nothing with a more successful record of accomplishment than Nature, so we look at how Nature does its business.

SESSION TWO: THE BUSINESS OF BIOLOGY

DNA IS SYMBIOTIC: BACTERIA IS SYMBIOTIC. BACTERIA FORMED INTO MULTI-CELLED LIFE FORMS.

MULTI-CELLED LIFE FORMS ARE SYMBIOTIC. BACTERIA CREATED: BACTERIA INVENTED: BACTERIA PIONEERED: BACTERIA DEVELOPED:

THE HUMAN BODY IS A SYMBIOTIC HOLARCHY. IF WE RAN OUR BODY IN THE SAME WAY WE RUN THE WORLD ECONOMY, WE WOULD ALL DIE.

The accomplishments of Nature and the elegant beauty of its complexities is an example to everyone. This session is about what Nature has accomplished.

SESSION THREE: HOW NATURE CONDUCTS BUSINESS

THE PROCESS OF NEGOTIATING SELF-INTEREST WITHIN THE WHOLE DYNAMIC: HEALTHY NEGOTIATION: COMMUNICATION, COMPROMISE AND TRANSFORMATION; YOUNG SPECIES AND MATURE SPECIES; COMPETITION AND COOPERATION; CYCLES OF DEVELOPMENT.

This session is about how Nature negotiates and how resolution develops according to natural cycles. The applications of this information to business become self-evident.

SESSION FOUR: SCULPTURING THE CORPORTATE CULTURE

THE NATURAL DEVELOPMENT OF THE CORPORATION: THE STOCKHOLDER'S HOLARCHY; THE QUADRUPLE BOTTOM LINE; CONSCIOUSNESS AND THE DIMENSIONS OF REALITY.

Those who become the giants of success in the future will be aligned with the natural stages of development of their business. They will include multiple bottom line frameworks and be aware of the role of consciousness in their business dynamics.

SESSION FIVE: THE ENFOLDED DIMENSION OF HYPERSPACE

NON-LOCALITY AND THE QUANTUM VIEW OF BUSINESS: THE HYPER-SPACIAL COUNTERPART OF THE COMPANY; THE BIOLOGY OF CON-SCIOUSNESS; COLLECTIVE CONSCIOUSNESS; THE HOLOGRAPHIC VIEW AND HOW TO EMPOWER POTENTIAL.

WHY RELATIONSHIPS ARE EVERYTHING: THE B.O.S.S. (BEING OF SYS-TEMS SYNERGY).

Understanding that business is quantum and holographic provides an advantage in the world of commerce. Aligning corporate mentality with the collective unveils hidden keys to success.

SESSION SIX: HOW TO TRANSFORM THE CORPORATION

A TOPOLOGY OF THE STAGES OF DEVELOPMENT OF BUSINESS: THE PO-TENTIALIZATION PROCESS FOR A CORPORATION; THE LESSONS OF NA-TURE; THE ESSENTIAL FEATURES OF A HEALTHY LIVING SYSTEM; SELF-CREATION AND SELF-MAINTENANCE; RESPONSE-ABILITY; COMMUNICA-TION; TRANSFORMATION; EMPOWERMENT; COORDINATION; BALANCE OF INTERESTS; RECIPROCITY; SHARING OF INFORMATION; HOW THE TRANSFORMATION PROCESS WORKS.

In a dynamic universe, businesses must be prepared for growth and development. There are natural stages through which a business develops and, once understood, growth can be planned for and implemented effectively and efficiently.

SESSION SEVEN: THE MATURE CORPORATION

ECOLOGICAL ETHICS: COMMUNITY INVOLVEMENT; THE COOPERATIVE SPECIES; THE IMPACT OF CONSCIOUSNESS.

The academy sponsors courses for corporations and businesses because, like any other subject, the underlying principles of corporate management and effective functioning are best understood as they are implemented. Individual success cannot be isolated from collective success.

Chapter Six

The Opportunities: Bringing the Future into the Present

T HE OPPORTUNITIES ARE ENDLESS. IF THEY ARE NOT IMMEDIATELY STARING YOU in the face, you can create them. Wherever you look, you can see potential waiting to unfold. You can choose a mission and manifest its fulfillment. Here are some examples:

Technology:

There are tens of thousands of technologies waiting to be brought to market. Each offers a significant service to humankind. Here are a few examples:

- *Solar paint* - just paint it on and you have solar cells that produce their own energy, even indoors.
- *Super batteries* - made of layers of carbon one molecule thick, these batteries are more than 200 times stronger than ours, weigh almost nothing and are environmentally clean.
- *Terabits of Information on discs no larger than a 50-cent piece* - These discs can hold all known information, including all movies, TV shows and all the books ever written.
- *Pattern recognition* - allows information to be instantly retrieved. It seeks and finds only what it is asked to find. Pattern recognizers can be placed in cars, planes, boats and other transportation devices, making accidents virtually impossible. They can be used for instant information retrieval in any circumstance.
- *Quantum computers* - both on and off at the same time and capable of nonlinear processing and self-organization working at super speeds.
- *Photonic resistors* - allow computers to run on light, not on electricity. Photonics is the wave of the future in the computer industry. They are 2,000 times faster than electric computers and they operate on normal light.
- *Spinner antennas* - allow information to travel on the echo of waves, providing a whole new arena of broadcasting and transceiving billions of digital information channels on a single transponder.
- *High speed processors* - work 28 times faster than the human brain for organization of information.
- *Super wheels* - never wear out, cannot be flattened, leave no trace off-road and can even travel over a wheat field and leave no evidence of ever having been there.
- *Torus pumps* - can pump anything, even wet cement, 120 stories high, stop and start to fill a single cup or pours tons a minute. Capable of "pumping" live people (firemen up into high rise buildings, rescuing potential victims), equipment and supplies without damage.
- *Vertical lift vehicles* - without propellers and can be built to any size from single person to jumbo jets.

- *High definition video cameras* - miniature with clear definition from a distance.
- *Alternative energy sources* - Solar energy holds new promise, but perhaps the most remarkable development is that of zero-point energy harmonics, allowing endless energy to be available in a suitcase - sized container.
- *New engines* - Ceramic - infused lightweight motors are 40 to 60 percent more efficient and pollutant - free and still run on gasoline or other oils. After more than a million miles of testing, there is no evidence of engine wear.
- *Electric vehicles* that have electric motors in their wheels and, with super batteries, can travel over 10,000 miles on a single charge, *Etc. Etc. Etc.*

Education

Some of the greatest leaps forward in human consciousness are showing up in the arena of education. They include the following examples:

- *Personal transceivers*: Every teacher and student carries a miniature personal transceiver capable of instant communication, multiple - processing and high - definition TV. A student can be tutored anywhere in the world.
- *Interactive compute-assisted course work*: From pre-birth to death, courses are becoming available on computer, allowing students to work through their education via interactive courses. High quality education available to everyone.
- *Direct experience*: Some classes take place aboard mobile ships; others offer direct visitation to countries being studied. Everything from farming to manufacturing can be obtained via direct experience within different cultures.
- *Future job simulation*: Students are trained for future jobs via simulation and direct visitation to industry or the work place.
- *Tutoring*: Students receive special tutoring in any subject from the best minds available. Senior citizens, teachers, older students, specialists, and even people in the workplace, with real experience, can tutor students interested in the subject.
- *New curriculum and classrooms*: Both the classroom and the curriculums are in the middle of a great transition. Educational philosophies are changing; teachers are looking for new and better ways to exchange information.
- *Home Education*: The Information Age provides access at home. Education is headed toward more family involvement, more home-centered school time and more practical applications, preparing for jobs of the future and distillation of information.
- *Earn as you learn*: Students have access to tutors and get paid as they trained for specific jobs. They also can create their own education programs according to market demand.

Information

This is an Information Age. Fifty years ago, half the jobs in America were agricultural. Forty-five percent were industrial and only five percent were information jobs. Now, more than fifty percent of all jobs are informational.

- *Smart card*: Credit cards that can tell when their owner is using them, knows the balance in the bank account and are secured against fraud.
- *Nano-technologies*: provide instant information on any subject to anyone in the world.
- *Personal transceivers*: provide shopping for anything, anywhere, at any time, in three-dimensional high definition TV personally adapted to your needs. If you want to purchase a dress in Paris, it is available in multiple colors, styles and prices that fit you to a T at the touch of a button.
- *Personalized banking*: 24 hours a day, 365 days a year you can access your bank, get credits for services rendered and establish new lines of credit through international coalitions.
- *Personal access to the arts*: Not only can you create your own art works but you can arrange for the finest art, music and entertainment to be wired directly into your home, via high definition video screens, placed on walls, interchangeable with real-to-life shows at any time.
- *Intelligent homes, transportation (cars, planes, boats, motorcycles, bikes, skate boards, etc.)*: all provide alternative power supplies (solar powered energy, zero-point energy, wind, water, etc.) and artificial intelligence, making travel and living a fail-free experience.

Manufacturing

With demilitarization, the large factories that are surrounded by communities of trained and intelligent personnel begin to decentralize. With the Information Age emerges a large, new, ambitious population seeking to make their place in the world.

- *Underutilized factories*: waiting production contracts, it is possible to put these people to work, retool the factories, and shift from a military society to a productive one.
- *Robotization*: allows mass production of new products with minimal people involvement.
- *New territories*: especially in developing countries, but also in unclaimed areas such as the ocean and deserts, where people can take the opportunity to participate, to develop self-sustaining communities, develop manufacturing capabilities and distribute new products.
- *Strategic networks*: provide more local coordination of resources, food and services to better solve the problems and unfold the potential "in our own back yard."
- *Extend our services*: international cooperation in manufacturing products. A simple toy may have its motor parts made in Japan, its plastics cast in Russia, assembly in Brazil and distribution out of Europe. An American firm may own it and its banking may come out of Canada. Networks can be co-located for transport efficiencies, and the personal transceivers can potentialize bioregional solutions with everyone involved!

Health

Technology is now available that provides high quality health care for everyone. These technologies include the following:

- *Non-invasive diagnostics*: of every disease; more than 6,000 toxins and even viral infections can be detected and effectively treated with alternative (homeopathic, dialysis, etc.) remedies.
- *Nutritional diagnostics*: depicts nutritional levels and shows exactly what vitamins or minerals the body needs at any given time.
- *Virtual reality integration*: Doctors create three-dimensional virtual realities of patient's body and bio-systems and integrate information from all diagnostic equipment in hospitals or out in the field.
- *Personal health monitoring*: Doctors and patients develop a personal health monitoring system. Equipped with personal transceivers, they maintain constant touch with each other for prevention, education and treatment.
- *Anti-aging*: via a new chelation process, the marrow of bones can be treated to significantly delay the aging process. It is estimated the process will allow people to live more than 400 years when combined with proper nutrition and exercise.
- *Cure of all viral, bacterial and fungal diseases*: a dialysis plus treatment allows the blood to be treated according to its specific disease, boosts the immune system and ends our fear of being infected by any virus (including AIDS, hepatitis, etc.) and any fungus or any bacteria.

Security

New pattern recognition sensors make home, office, cars and countries more secure.

- *Detection*: High - definition video cameras capable of seeing at long distances provide instant recognition and detection at airports, banks, hospitals, borders and other security facilities.
- *Instant response*: Satellite information correlation provides the opportunity for quick response to potential criminal acts.
- *Scanners*: New, low-level neutron bombardments make possible the instant scanning of, for example, airplanes. This means a 747 can be rolled into a scanner hanger, scanned and the computer will immediately detect even the slightest flaw in anything – even a single bolt deep inside of the machine.
- *Intelligent communities*: "Intelligent" communities, where homes, streets and public facilities are patrolled and programmed for security and maximum convenience. Homes are automatically secured and can only be opened by those authorized.
- *Undetectable chips*: Cars, boats, cargo, even your own television set, can be implanted with identification chips that transmit an invisible signal. If stolen or lost, it can immediately be found.

Economics

- With the world at our fingertips, we can provide economic opportunities for everyone. Yes, *everyone*.
- *Global access*: Local products can be marketed first locally, and then worldwide. New trade agreements are possible between individuals.
- *Direct purchase and delivery*: Local products can be purchased direct and delivered within hours, anywhere in the world. The cost savings can be as much as 50 percent.
- *Comprehensive coverage*: Every community service and product can be made available. Those willing to do the work can meet market demands. Business clubs can be organized to teach local people how to conduct business and meet market demands. Alliances can be negotiated between local and regional governments providing assistance and resources to those who seek economic independence.

Ecology

- *Monitoring*: It is now possible to provide global monitoring. This means we can detect dysfunction such as the disease of a single tree in a forest, dumping of pollution into the ocean and streams, and even minute traces of pollution in the air.
- *Overcoming toxic waste*: It is possible to create a sustainable plasmic field from an alternating and direct electrical current. The temperatures reached are able to transform any toxic waste (including nuclear waste) and the only byproduct is pure energy and nano carbons. The nano carbons can be used to create all kinds of things including super capacity batteries.
- *Advanced warning*: We can detect disasters and take preventative measure before the situation gets out of hand. Earthquakes can be detected 48 hours in advance via satellite. Weather warnings, asteroid detection, even troop movements in a war zone, can be detected on a worldwide basis.
- *Keeping the balance*: From satellites, it is possible to detect over-fishing, over-forestation and destruction of rain forests. It is possible to identify disruptions in the food chain, detect low ozone levels and other disruptions in the complex symbiosis of life. It becomes a matter of public consciousness and public action. The balance of life can be restored and maintained on the planet.

Summary

It is true that there is no absolute reality waiting "out there" to be discovered. What is "waiting to be discovered" is the powerful position we have as part of a living, dynamic, conscious multidimensional universe where everything is made of information and everything is connected. We are part of a holographic system that takes on this four-dimensional form in space and time but we are actually much more. We get to choose the form our reality takes. We are, in reality, co-creators of life. We get to choose!

So - Let us choose! Let us choose our part, the games we want to play, and let us manifest what we know, deep down inside ourselves. This is our mission in life. Let us integrate the past and the future into the now. Let the harmonics of our soul sing our song and let us dance our dance of life together.

I cannot write your song nor do your dance but I can sing along and dance with you this dance of life. If we discover anything, let us discover that how we live on this planet is part of the Covenant we make. At least let us learn about our Covenant.

There are certain dimensions of our Covenant that have captured my interest: particle, wave and presence; the implicate order; the holographic nature of consciousness and how everything works in harmony. I have looked at the potential that exists in the field right now and, in response, I have decided to place *form* around certain of its possibilities. I, like you, am a manifester and, as such, I am personally involved in choosing to potentialize certain possibilities. I understand there are particle aspects to this project, wave aspects to it and that it comes from our Holodynamic state of being. From my particle mind, for example, I am involved in the following:

Technology: I served as CEO to an international company whose mission is to bring technology to market. Our first project was to develop and distribute personal transceivers and to launch a new satellite system to provide for their global use. I am now working on using the super-plasmic arch to provide solutions to environmental pollution. I am also working on the Wellness Program for curing all viral, bacteria and fungal diseases.

Information: I am a member of the Academy of Natural Science of Russia. I also serve as Director of the International Academy of Holodynamics. I seek the best information available in order to help me unfold the greatest potential possible in life.

Education: I am convinced that the most important aspect of education is to teach Holodynamics. Everyone can become an advocate of the whole dynamic of reality. Without the ability to access our true natures and our Full Potential Self, as well as monitor our holodynes and shift our field dynamics, it does not matter what technology or programs we develop. The use of any new technologies will still be run by our potentially lethal holodynes. The potential applications of new technologies will be limited by our own thinking. The principles and processes of Holodynamics hold the keys to shifting our personal and collective consciousness.

This is not just another theory. Over 3 decades of research and applications have demonstrated Holodynamics to be successful in solving some of the most complex problems on the planet. So this approach works and the Holodynamic framework correlates with the best information from the most current sciences. Holodynamics creates a new state of consciousness. It's about "the whole dynamic." We can learn to use our new technologies *within* our society of new consciousness. Only then can we truly succeed in unfolding our fullest potential. So I *teach* Holodynamics and educate others teachers to teach Holodynamics.

Health: It is possible to bring noninvasive, personal health monitoring to every person via the personal transceivers. We are in the process of establishing Wellness Centers that have a "healing" aspect to their education program. In bringing new technology to market, we also bring the new technology of health to market. Noninvasive diagnostics, homeopathic and alternative healing processes and nutritional monitoring, along with integrated, three-dimensional diagnostics and medical supervision, are part of the program.

Freedom: Freedom (as a state of being) is possible Holodynamically. Once your mind, heart and soul are free, it is possible to arrange networks and alliances for economic and cultural freedom. In order to accomplish this, we can establish banking and other alliances to help you create financial and cultural freedom. It becomes possible to set not only your own prime conditions but the prime conditions for whole communities and even countries.

Starting in my own back yard: I have learned that I must start in my own back yard. I will not touch a piece of real estate without first knowing that it will be cared for in a responsible way. I am convinced that the land is a living thing, the home has a soul of its own, and trees and plants can communicate. The biosphere is conscious. Therefore, I start in my own back yard. I make sure every part of the landscape reflects a field in which the plants can fulfill their own potential. At the same time, I want the land to reflect the beauty I am and so I add my own "fingerprint," so to speak, to the property and to the community.

Within any region, it is possible to restore the natural life of plants. It is possible to introduce new species, ones that will enhance the productivity and beauty of the living space. I support research in and encourage self-sufficiency and agricultural consciousness. In this regard, I plant, in my yard, those plants that bear fruit or food, medicines and herbs of all sorts. When the soil becomes depleted, I am interested in bioconversion processes and helping the soil maintain self-sufficiency. Since plants grow in natural communities, I am interested in establishing biological balance, planting in ecological complementary fashion and allowing plants to blend and protect each other.

Expanding this same philosophy to people, I am interested in establishing the latest information systems, as well as education, economic and health programs. This all starts with the teaching of Holodynamics and thus I teach it. I join with others of like mind and we work together as a team, planting both seeds and ideas, stimulating growth both on the land and in the people. It is fun. It is dynamic. It is life!

I never lose my focus on global conditions. My *being* feels the same about the world as is it does about my own back yard. Since information organizes from micro to macro, my own back yard reflects outward. If we can all clean up our own back yard, the rest of the world will follow.

No one was born alone and no one dies alone. We may believe in separation and play the separation games but, in reality, we have all made the Covenant. The essence of the Covenant is that we play the games in order to manifest who we are. Who are you? What do you choose? I promise to love and support you in whatever you choose. I may not choose to play the game you are playing but I support you in the right you have to play the game and accept the consequences.

I want to emphasize that you do not need me or anyone else. My particle mind thinks I did all this without having my own prime conditions set. I did this without direct support from wife, family or my old friends. I did this regardless of my religion, education or community support. Nothing, nothing at all, can stand between my Full Potential Self and me. I have the right to choose and to manifest what I consider to be the fullest potential and the best deal possible.

I choose to face what others consider unsolvable problems. I choose to go beyond the collective mentality, not because I am a rebel but because I care. I care enough to go beyond conformity and consensus. I choose to go for the fullest potential possible in every situation. I choose to look beyond the myths and cultural walls about drug abuse, mental illness, maximum-security prisoners, juvenile "delinquents" and even the Cold War. I choose to make a difference and I invite you to do the same. Why? Well, for one thing, the consequences are well worth the effort. For another, teams work! We can move beyond war and terror. We can become the solution.

Anyone familiar with wave mechanics knows that the frequency of any wave in harmony with another wave is squared. Thus a holodyne, resonating in quantum coherence with another person's holodynes, squares the strength of their information field. The impact of my view of the future is squared when one other person views the future in the same way.

In other words, I am equal to one. Two people, in harmony with each other, are equal to four. Three people are equal in strength to nine (3 squared = 9), four are equal to 16, and etc. In a world of six billion people, it is estimated that 80,000 people could affect the field with sufficient strength to create their own reality. When I hold the fields for a certain future, others of like mind are drawn to that field and, by their own choice, they become part of the natural reinforcement of the field. The field grows exponentially. At the same time, I know that all it takes is one person to reset the entire collective field.

I can look back upon the past, using my Full Potential Self as my guide, and I can "relive" the transition from oneness into separation. It occurred individually and collectively. The oneness was evident in ancient tribal communities. They knew the Holodynamic nature of the universe; spoke to the plants and animals and lived in harmonic balance for many thousands of years. Then we invented separation. We invented dominance and hierarchical power systems with clear authority structures. We invented trade and commerce; and the use of money as a symbol of power and the right to control. We invented the conquest of other tribes, of women and of ideologies. We invented divinization, masculine patriarchal control and enforced evangelism.

We created the theological idealism of complete absorption of other cultures and tribes and, along with it, we invented scorched-earth agriculture. We created both science and religion to support our view and, then, from the tribal societies of Gigamesh, we touched the Syrians, Greeks, Romans, Hebrews, Arabs, Vikings, Turks, Huns and the imperial Europeans of Britain, France, Portugal, Belgium and Holland. This same ideology and invented society touched the Americas, the Incas and Mayans and spread into Africa with the Zulu, China, Japan, Korea and even the Brahmins of India. Every tribal society that stood in their way was exterminated.

The result is a collective consciousness that has its own event horizon. We believe in growth, expansion and more and more control over more and more resources. We consume far more than we produce and we are halfway through the consumption of the world's oil supply. We are now looking for alternative energy sources with the same intention, to conquer and control, to charge others to use the energy and keep them in eternal bondage so those at the top of the pyramid of power can have the freedom they choose at the expense of others. It is a system out of balance and it cannot do anything but turn upon itself as it reaches the boundaries of its own event horizon.

The key to life rests in the whole dynamic of the past and future as it integrates into the now. The new technologies, new sciences and new Information Age bring to the public the opportunity to adopt the wisdom of our ancestors and apply it today. We can visit the future, see how every problem came to be solved and begin to implement those solutions now. We become the solution by choice. It begins in our own back yard. It begins within our micro systems and within the community of our holodynes, extending outward from there. Personal transformation precedes public transformation. In the future, I see, everyone having their own prime conditions set. The entire biosphere achieves a harmonic balance. I choose this future.

I realize now that my own journey could have been a lot easier. I could have set my prime conditions for family, for each program, and for my associates and myself. There was a lot of work, sacrifice and struggle involved. These were my holodynes and, thanks to my Holodynamic friends, I am overcoming these old habits. I am sharing this with you so that you may see we are all in a similar boat. We are all astronauts on this planet earth and we all have holodynes.

The Dance of Life, these manuals, other materials and courses are designed so we can "call home", be in contact with our source, and accept that inner state of being as our own state of being here. From that state of being, we sense the living principles by which life works. We can create a new set of metaphors, stories, rituals, dances, social graces, internal and external acts of unconditional love and a new respect for others because we know their past, future and all the parallel worlds in which we live and love each other. We come to understand the deep underlying principles of life.

Understanding these principles makes our journey here easier and life takes on more meaning. We begin to experience our true nature and our togetherness with each other and with nature. It all starts with personal *presence*.

Kirk Rector wrote a story about presence. I thought you might find it interesting so, with his permission, I have included it in the Appendix A.

We will be exploring these *living principles* in the next manual. See you there!

APPENDIX A

THE MYTH OF ADONI

By

J. Kirk Rector
J.D., M.B.A., M.P.A.

Translated into Russian from English
By Larisa Harchenko

Chapter One

An Ascended Master Chooses a Vacation

It's an interesting mental exercise to turn the whole game upside down: The problem is not how to free oneself from the mass level to get enlightened. The real question is if you are a completely free and self-determined being, how did you lock yourself into a body to play games on the material plane? How did you get yourself and others to agree to this game? How did you get it to be compulsive?

Thaddeus Golas, *The Lazy Man's Guide to Enlightenment.*

The "Self," on the other hand, is a God - image, or at least cannot be distinguished from one. Of this the early Christian spirit was not ignorant, otherwise Clement of Alexandria could never have said that he who knows himself, knows God.

Carl Jung, *Aion: Researches into the Phenomenology of the Self.*

As the greatest politicians, artists, spiritual leaders, and even scientists know in their gut, only new myth can inspire creative cultural change.

Richard Heinberg, *New Myth, New Culture*

Be humble, for you are made of earth.
Be noble, for you are made of stars.

Serbian proverb

Once upon a time, there was an ascended master named Adoni.

Adoni dwelt from eternity to eternity at the heart of the great M31 galaxy that appears in the constellation Andromeda. There, suspended in hyperspace, beyond time, he enjoyed all power, all knowledge and all love - as one.

This oneness was borne in the holographic wholeness of his infinite consciousness, which was aware of all things and resonated in harmony with the unified field.

Adoni spent most of his eternity in loving counsel with twelve other Ascended Masters presiding over the 300 billion star systems within M31, maintaining powerful peace in that region of the universe. All things remained in infinite abundance, harmony and joy, as is the natural condition prevailing across most of the universe.

But, after spending several eternities in this great oneness and keeping everything in such profound order, it was decided that Adoni deserved a vacation.

Now this was a bit of a dilemma. Where would a great, all - powerful ascended master go for vacation? And how do you vacate from omnipresence, omnipotence, omniscience and all that love?

Adoni felt this issue needed his focused attention. Stepping out of the eternity for a moment, he switched on his "now - consciousness," his "current time self," a friendly, unassuming personality, and called up the Cosmic Travel Agency.

"Hello!" began Adoni. "I'm an ascended master about to take a vacation from my position on the Council in M31. What excursion packages for masters are you currently offering?"

"Oh, thank you for choosing our agency!" a pleasant woman's voice began. "We've been anticipating your call. Yes, we offer wonderful packages that might intrigue an ascended master!" As she spoke, a selection of colorful travel brochures instantly appeared in Adoni's hands.

"Good, tell me about them," said Adoni as he began to scrutinize each pamphlet sequentially with his left brain.

"To start," began the agent, "notice the stunning Golden Planet of Success. Here we arrange an awards ceremony in your honor, acknowledging all the great good you've done across the Andromeda galaxy. We invite each of your ascended master friends from beyond time and space, and hold an awesome party! We have interplanetary rock bands, celestial celebrities and…"

"Thanks so much!" interrupted Adoni. "But, you know, I don't really need all that. It's a vacation I'm after."

"Oh, of course!" agreed the agent. "I just want you to know that this party option is available. Now, for a vacation," she continued, "in the second folder, we offer the Green Planet of Serenity. There you lie amid tall grass in the ethereal shade and luxuriate in refreshing mist blowing from countless extraterrestrial waterfalls. No one bothers you for eons of time. You can enjoy a well-deserved rest."

"Oh, that would be wonderful," confided Adoni, examining the green holographic renderings on the folder. "But it's not exactly what I'm looking for. Do you have something more… exotic?"

"Exotic - certainly!" said the agent. Suddenly, a brilliant red bolt of lighting split the unified field and the next pamphlet appeared in Adoni's hands. "Here's the Scarlet Planet of Passion!"

"Wow!" exclaimed Adoni.

"On this planet, you rendezvous with your cosmic sweetheart and melt together into sheer, exotic ecstasy - creating vast fountains of love energy, which become the origin of life everywhere. Wouldn't that be delightful!"

"Yes," agreed Adoni, with a bit of hesitation. "But, you see, I did that last vacation."

"Oh. Well, then," paused the agent, "what else are you looking for?"

"Something very unusual. You know, something you don't find in every universe."

"Aha! I suspected as much!" admitted the agent. "But I wanted you to first examine some alternatives before I presented you the very spot I hoped you might choose."

Adoni Learns of the Blue Planet.

Suddenly, another pamphlet appeared in Adoni's hands.

"Here's quite a unique retreat," she began. "We've received lots of glowing reports on it lately. It's the Blue Planet!"

"The Blue Planet?" responded Adoni curiously.

"Yes, a terrestrial sphere set in three-dimensional space at a rustic location way out in the country near the outer edge of a medium - sized galaxy."

"Only three dimensions!" exclaimed Adoni.

"Yes!" continued the agent. "Can you imagine! If you collapse the quantum potential field down to that tight a level, it creates a unique finite perception of reality. Your senses only pick up up/down, across and sideways, with a very limited spectrum of colors and shapes. You must live between a particle/wave, manifest/unmanifest world, which separates your awareness into two parts - conscious and unconscious - and time continuum into three: past, present and future."

"Interesting. But why would I want to visit such a place? It sounds too restricted and rather drab!" Adoni asked.

"Restricted, yes; but drab, no!" explained the agent. "Take a look at the brochure. Notice how abundant nitrogen in the atmosphere imparts that rich blue color, while the surface temperature hovers around the vapor point of water, so you get all sorts of colorful meteorology - see! The profuse water also supports a wonderful assortment of oxy-hydro-carbon life systems utilizing DNA. Notice all the possible life forms!"

"Wouldn't all that water erode away most of the terrestrial features?"

"No," continued the agent. "Of course, there are large oceans. But you'll also find beaches, wetlands, prairies, forests, mountains and deserts. Plus, the planet's rotational axis is not perfectly aligned, so it progresses through seasons of warm and cold each year, creating a great variety of weather conditions and interesting adaptations by the life forms. The effects on the landscape, flora and fauna are stunning."

The agent showed Adoni some more pictures, which somehow began to appeal to him.

"Well, I must agree, it does appear exotic! Quite a vacation spot." confirmed Adoni. "But this restricted environment still concerns me. What could an ascended master do there?"

"Oh, that's the exciting part!" responded the agent with increasing enthusiasm. "You undergo a unique experience called: 'The Separation Vacation!'"

"The *what?*" asked Adoni.

"The Separation Vacation!" she repeated. "As you enter the third dimension, you undergo amnesia, and get separated from everything - from your awareness of all time, all space, all power, all knowledge, all love - and most of all, from yourself."

"Separated from myself?" asked Adoni.

"Yes" she said. "The 3-D effect conceals all your power, knowledge, and love, deep in your unmanifest subconscious, blocking your access to it. Thus, most of your ascended master powers stay either inaccessible or all canceled out in negative dynamics."

"Wow - separation from all power, knowledge, love! Suffering from amnesia and locked in negative dynamics! What a novel idea," Adoni mused. "Now you've really got my interest!"

"Of course, that's why I saved it for last" the agent said. "There are only a few places in the universe where you can enjoy such a vacation. It took us quite a while to develop this planet, over 4 billion years. But we've tested it thoroughly, and as I said, we are now getting lots of great reports from visitors telling us this resort provides all the vacation enjoyment they expected, and more."

"More? What do you mean?" inquired Adoni.

"Oh, while on holiday upon the Blue Planet you get to play all sorts of games: each a variation of a planetary, multidimensional and transpersonal 'hide-and-seek," she replied.

"Hide-and-seek?" Adoni questioned.

"Since you are separated from yourself, you get to hunt around for yourself again. You spend your entire vacation trying to rediscover all your unconscious power, knowledge and love - all your immortality and all your multidimensional connections with the universe. Sometimes it takes several lifetimes."

"But isn't it dangerous?" asked Adoni, forgetting himself for a moment.

"How could it be?" continued the agent, surprised at Adoni's concern. "Your Full Potential Self is always present in the quantum potential field. It guides the entire process from higher dimensions. So there's no way this vacation can actually hurt you. It's only your now - consciousness locked in three dimensions that loses track of everything. You roam around saying: 'Where am I?' 'Who am I?' 'What's going on here?' And you develop all sorts of outlandish philosophical explanations to figure out what's happening. Now doesn't that sound like fun!"

"You bet!" exclaimed Adoni, and he considered the possibilities. "Can I be anything I want: a man, a woman, a pauper, a king? Can I suffer disease, feel pain, make other people and myself miserable! That sort of thing?"

"Certainly!" said the agent "All the other vacationers on the Blue Planet are just like you, ascended masters on vacation! You can have a lot of fun with your eternal friends. Plus, looking down upon yourselves from the higher dimensions together, your Full Potential Selves will be able to enjoy observing all these exotic experiences."

"Oh, that does sound entertaining!" replied Adoni

Then Adoni paused. "Yet, again, what's the point. I mean - underneath everything is always love! Isn't that apparent there?"

"No, the amnesia and separation hide it." She explained "This planet is one of the few places in the universe where omnipresent love is not immediately obvious. Only over time does your three-dimensional consciousness learn what the universe is about. You rediscover it, like new - all bright and beautiful, deep in your subconscious! Then you can overcome the amnesia and transform the negative dynamics."

"But how do I rediscover myself if I and everyone around me are suffering from so much amnesia?" Adoni asked incredulously.

"That's really no problem," the agent reassured him. "Every now and then your Full Potential Self will whisper little clues to you. 'Look at this.' 'Read that book.' 'Talk to that person over there.' 'Attend that seminar!' Opportunities are always popping up, if you are observant. Each time you rediscover something about yourself. It's a great experience. You'll see. Then near the end, you'll coach yourself to transform all these negative dynamics into their powerful positive potential. Like magic!"

"Really!" Adoni said, astonished.

"Yes." confirmed the agent, as she began to speak slower. "And by the time you've finish a few lifetimes, you're all enlightened. You appreciate everything about yourself and love everyone again. You're refreshed and ready to return to universal bliss."

"You know, this idea of a Separation Vacation sounds more and more like what I want," confessed Adoni. "How long can I stay?"

"As long as you choose. Each lifetime is usually less than 100 years. And since time is relative, you can have as many lives as you want," she said.

"Wonderful!" he explained.

"You enter the third dimension," continued the agent, "in whatever century you want - in past, present, future or parallel worlds. You live wherever on the planet you wish. And you come back to oneness whenever your Full Potential Self chooses."

Adoni paused again, this time for more than just a moment. He imagined this unique, exotic vacation with all its possibilities, all the adventures and the fun he would have. It all flashed immediately before his omniscient mind in the quantum potential field. It was irresistible.

"All right, I'll go!" he declared. "I'll leave immediately. Charge all the expenses on my Universal Credit Card!"

Adoni Takes the Trip.

So Adoni agreed to take his holiday on the Blue Planet, experiencing the Separation Vacation in three dimensions and playing transpersonal hide-and-seek.

"Now, what must I do to prepare?" Adoni asked.

"First, fill in your answers to the questions in the Blue Planet brochure," explained the agent. "You'll find a full questionnaire on the back. This includes a description of the kind of body you want and the mental conditions you'd like."

"Body?" he asked, somewhat confused.

The agent then explained in more detail, "That's one of those three-dimensional material projections of your Full Potential Self, with special faculties designed for the Blue Planet. The brochure outlines everything. It even explains how to break up your collective universal intelligence into consciousness and unconsciousness, and then further into your different holodynes."

"My what?" he inquired.

"Don't worry, it's all in the brochure," offered the agent.

Adoni agreed, "Okay, I'll read and fill it out."

"Good. Next we'll arrange the trip for you. The transport vehicle will arrive to pick you up as soon as you're prepared; and you'll be telepathed to the threshold between hyperspace and the Blue Planet, where you'll be met by those who will explain what to do next. Thanks for your business, and good luck!" The agent's voice vanished.

But Adoni hardly noticed; he was already busy preparing. He found that the questionnaire listed everything he might want, with little boxes to check it all off. So he continued in his now - consciousness.

At first, he decided that he'd go for just one lifetime and see how he enjoyed it, then maybe sign up for more. But he had trouble selecting whether to be a man or a woman, so he decided to experience two lifetimes, one for each.

It was also difficult choosing where on the Blue Planet he wanted to live. There were great cities and small towns, even isolated countryside - and so many different languages and cultures, with so many traditions.

In order to make up his mind, he switched into his full - potential - future mode. He chose all he desired to do, have and be as they already are in the future, then regressed time back into the choices that made this future possible. Finally back into now - consciousness, it was then easy to fill out the questionnaire.

When he concluded, he had chosen a small town with a long established culture and parents he already knew well as associate ascended masters, who he learned were also taking a vacation on the Blue Planet. He'd go as a man his first trip, then as a woman his second.

Adoni was just about finished filling in these blanks when suddenly he heard a steep roar. The transport vehicle had arrived.

It was a massive set of resonating frequencies, all coherent in perfect harmony. As it approached, it adjusted up to Adoni's threshold frequency and then surrounded him with violet-golden light. Within no time, Adoni was absorbed into the resonance of the transport vehicle and prepared for hyperspace travel.

Instantly the local gravity waves went into phase lock and a synthetic black hole opened up. The vehicle abruptly disappeared with a flash of light into the black hole.

As it sped along through the singularity, Adoni had only a moment to complete the questionnaire. "Yes, I'd like to have some diseases," he thought, so he checked off several. "Yes, I'll be married and have children. That will cause lots of anxiety." He marked the appropriate spaces. "Maybe I'll join a church or political party, that's always a waste of energy!"

Time slowed down to nothing, then started up again on the other side of the singularity, but to Adoni it all elapsed in one flash as the transport vehicle approached its destination.

Chapter Two

Adoni is Greeted

"Some things, Ivan, you described very well and satirically," Berlioz was saying, "for example, the birth of Jesus, the son of God, but the fact is that a whole host of sons of Gods were born even before Jesus, like, say, Phoenician Adonis, the Phrygian Attis, the Persian Mithras. But in short, none of them, including Jesus, were ever born or existed, and so, instead of describing his birth or, say, the coming of the Magi, you should describe the nonsense that was said about all this. Otherwise your account seems to suggest that he really was born!..."

Mikhail Bulgakov, *The Master and Margarita*

"There are seven planes in all, seven planes, each one consisting of many levels, one of them being the plane of recollection. On that plane you are allowed to collect your thoughts. You are allowed to see your life that has just passed. Those of the higher levels are allowed to see history."

Katherine, patient under hypnosis of Brian Weiss, M.D., in *Many Lives Many Masters*

The wizard watches the world come and go, but his soul dwells in realms of light.

Deepak Chopra in *The Way of the Wizard.*

As the transport vehicle got within visual contact of the Blue Planet, it suddenly came to a halt. Adoni was concerned.

"What's happened?" he asked, almost aloud.

Looking out the portal, he discovered where he was. Below him spun the blue orb. It was truly beautiful. At this range he could distinguish all sorts of colors. Yes, there were wide blue seas, gracious green and ruddy brown continents, all with dancing white cloud cover. Adoni noticed it was surrounded by a third-dimensional barrier, a kind of threshold that now must to be crossed through one of numerous tunnels in the time-space continuum. The vehicle awaited his command.

The effect of the planet's gravity was also apparent. There was a subtle, highly pitched buzzing vibration as the various dimensions tended to pull themselves apart and Adoni could already feel some of his multidimensional self separating. He noticed he lacked some of his instant, all-knowing, ascended master omniscience as he continued to gaze outside. In fact, he felt a little dizzy!

Then something wonderful happened. Violet-golden light began to gather in front of him. The light was faint at first but continued to grow in intensity.

Suddenly a group of ascended masters like himself appeared within this light, which Adoni realized was the resonance of their own transport vehicles surrounding each of them.

Adoni was fresh from finishing all the choices in the questionnaire; so he was surprised to find among this group so many results of his choices. He recognized his prospective parents, his future wife and children, his close friends and even his worst enemies - all the people that would either affect him or who he would affect on his vacation. They looked very peaceful, as all ascended masters do, and they seemed to wait for Adoni to speak.

"Hello. Don't I know you all from somewhere?" Adoni asked with a smile.

"Well, certainly," said the master nearest Adoni, smiling back. "I'm the Full Potential Self of your father to-be! This is the Full Potential of your expectant mother. These are your family and friends, as well as all your enemies. We're currently serving as the "Masters on the Threshold," and you have entered your Place of Planning. Welcome!"

"Oh what a pleasure!" Adoni exclaimed.

They all stepped out of their transport vehicles and made one large group surrounded by the violet-golden light. The love and understanding shared by this group irradiated and enveloped Adoni.

Now his mother spoke. "This is where you plan your life, my dear. It's your last omniscient act before your now - consciousness descends from hyperspace into the third dimension and suffers amnesia. I'll soon prepare a three-dimensional body for you on the Blue Planet."

"That's very unselfish of you!" said Adoni.

"But before you go down, we've all come to coordinate with you so you get what you really want and so do we," she said.

"How thoughtful!" he mused.

Adoni Observes Planet Life

Next, these Masters on the Threshold began to outline to Adoni some experiences he could expect on the Blue Planet. Together they looked down through the clouds.

For a few moments, it was difficult for Adoni to distinguish the planet's inhabitants from all the vegetation and landforms. But soon the movements of the people, as well as their thoughts and desires, became more discernible. Adoni scrutinized these surface inhabitants with great interest.

"Oh, so many of them are unhappy!" he observed. "Would you please explain this to me. I think my trip has fragmented some of my omniscience."

"Yes, that's why we're here to meet you," said the master, his father. "We'll explain everything. First, as you can see, most of the vacationers on the Blue Planet take life very seriously."

"But I thought they only play games!"

"Oh that's true. Yet look how they've identified themselves with their games," he said. "They've lost their cosmic oversight as well as the transcendent bliss we masters enjoy."

"I see," said Adoni, as he kept observing. "I'm sure I'll lose a lot of my bliss too. I expect that's part of the vacation. Would you tell me more about these games they are playing."

"Gladly," continued his father. "As the travel agent told you, each game is a version of hide-and-seek. Some people lose themselves in existential depression and simply play 'Life is Meaningless.' It's superb fun being so hopeless. There's only a few places in the universe you can do that."

"Then there's 'Life is a Cruel Punishment,'" his father continued. "You get into a pattern of suffering.-the Via Dolorosa. Your parents are abusive; God is cruel; the government unjust; the economy unfair; and everybody unforgiving. You believe you were born to suffer. So you do!"

Adoni's future father paused for a moment, and Adoni could feel vicariously some of the suffering those below him were experiencing. "What a curious game," Adoni thought. "Yet maybe I'd enjoy it. They certainly are!"

Then his mother took up where his father left off. "Maybe you'd like: 'Life is a Perilous Test?'" she suggested. "You think you're on probation, or being given your one chance to pass the exam of life. If you pass, you'll be eternally rewarded. But if you fail, oh, eternal damnation!"

"Boy, what jeopardy!" exclaimed Adoni with a wide grin.

His mother began to smile with him. "And there's more," she said. "How about: 'Life is a Challenging School.' Here you relearn the things you already innately know, thinking it's all new! Or how about: 'Life is a Sacred Mission.' You go on a great and noble quest. With trumpets, drums and flags you take on the forces of evil, or despotism, or slavery, or ignorance, and thus spend yourself in a great cause - only to discover later that everyone was actually fine. All you were doing was playing with each other, to discover one another's true selves."

"Doesn't anyone on the planet have conscious fun?" Adoni asked.

"Certainly!" spoke up his father. "Some play 'Life is Discovery!' or 'Life is Joy!' and even 'Life is Love!' If you look, you'll find that same blissful condition we experience everywhere in the universe. But down there, the majority of us want to have fun by being miserable."

"Yes," confessed Adoni. "Actually, that's one reason I chose this place. Misery, and then the great fulfillment that self-discovery brings, coming out of misery back into awareness and love."

"Well, sooner or later all the beings on the Blue Planet begin to approach life as a vacation for ascended masters; and finally understand how it's all set up for discovering themselves again, all unfolding their Full Potential Selves." he said "But it usually takes several lifetimes to reach that point."

"So I see," says Adoni.

The Blue Planet continued to turn below them, as they paused again to enjoy the mass movement of millions of ascended masters below, all separated from their higher selves, playing the games of life.

Adoni's father continued. "While under amnesia, look at the major strategies we masters use as we enjoy our vacation games. There's the 'Fear Tactic' in all its manifestations - anger, insecurity, manipulation, force, dominance, victimization, rules and roles, unethical activity, unscrupulousness, even tyranny! Can you see that down there?"

"Yes, I certainly do!" observed Adoni.

"There's the 'Segregation Maneuver,'" continued his father, "that disconnects and divides life into sections - infancy, childhood, adolescence, adult, single, married, divorced, middle age, elderly."

"Notice the 'Polarization Device,'" suggested his mother. "One part of the whole is set against another part. These form opposing sides in many of the games."

"Oh," added his father, "there are so many polarizations!"

"Like what?" questioned Adoni.

"Well, look down and see," his father directed, catching a long celestial breath. "You'll find mind-body, self-other, humankind-nature," he began. "Also male - female, child - parent, student - teacher, young - old, us - them, friend - enemy, love - hate, power - weakness, work - play, management - labor, public - private, objective - subjective, logic - intuition, good - bad and even life - death; to name a few!"

"Wow!" exclaimed Adoni.

"Can you see how each polarization creates a game of opposing parts?" continued his father. "Notice how neither side understands the other, nor how the whole could include them both."

"Yes, that's quite obvious from up here," observed Adoni.

"Also notice the `Projection Trick,'" His mother added. "Watch how people deny part of their inner polarization, and then project that denied part out onto other people. It's a curious compulsion of the inhabitants on the Blue Planet. They usually remain conscious of only what they consider their positive traits, and project their negatives. You too will find yourself unconsciously projecting most of your negative traits onto others and blaming them."

"This is really tricky!" noted Adoni.

"Yes," his father advised. "And it goes hand-in-hand with all the powerful addictions you can suffer."

"What do you mean?"

"Whenever you believe that some force beyond your own inner power is necessary to bring you happiness, you project that force upon all sorts of things outside you."

"Like what?" asked Adoni.

"Oh, on drugs, money, gambling, government, church, family, God, religion or even success. You can be obsessed with any of them," his father suggests. "You can devote your whole life to pursuing your obsession. But you're always left unfulfilled - because, as you know, happiness only comes from inside you."

"Right," agreed Adoni. "But what about gender? I notice the brochure allowed me to choose to live either as a man or a woman, but not both - that's a polarization - only one sex per trip. Is that true?" questioned Adoni.

"Yes," agreed his mother. "Sex is one of the more intriguing games on the Blue Planet! The third dimension simply divides your full life force and capacity for physical pleasure and inner harmony into male and female halves, hiding one half in your subconscious while emphasizing the other half in your physical body. Thus you feel polarized and believe you own only one half."

"It seems very bewildering," observed Adoni.

"Certainly. You wander around much of your life obsessed with the idea that someone out there is your other half. It's great for perpetuating the species and fills your life with endless games. And there are all sorts of varieties to be played: heterosexual, homosexual, bisexual, asexual! Plus there's the 'battle of the sexes;' the 'repression and denigration of sex,' as well as the 'exaltation and sanctification of sex..' It's fun to watch!" Again, she smiled.

117

"All these negative games are in fact caused by psychological states we call 'downdrafts,'" explained his father. "It's like getting caught in a gust of wind that whirls you out of balance and into disorder."

"That's in contrast to positive, 'updraft' states," added his mother, "which would lead us into equilibrium and well-being."

"Exactly," his father continued. "But actually, in the end, both of these mental states work together - the updrafts and downdrafts and synthesizing into a great whole. Each side contributes part of the larger fullness."

Finally, his father described the six basic arenas or stages where the games are played on the Blue Planet: the physical arena, the personal arena, the interpersonal arena, the social systems arena, the arena of principles, and the universal arena.

"Thus each of these six arenas has its own variety of entertaining pastimes," he concluded.

"How remarkable!" commented Adoni. Then he paused. He was beginning to feel quite dizzy again. He recognized this was the result of the intense three-dimensional gravity nearby. So he focused his attention and asked more questions to remain clear.

"Actually, it all seems too confusing." Adoni struggled to express his thoughts. "I mean, how can anyone make it through so much chaos?"

"Well, of course it's all confusing at first," explained his father. "But remember, you're an ascended master on vacation - you have great innate wisdom and power just below the surface of your consciousness mind. Plus, your Full Potential stands ready on this threshold to assist and enlighten your consciousness down on the Blue Planet at any time you ask."

"Your Full Potential will whisper through your intuition just what you need to know, just what you need to do, at just the right time - if you will just listen!" added his mother.

"Oh, the travel agent mentioned that. But will I really be able to communicate that readily with my higher self, despite all the amnesia?" asked Adoni.

"Well, it gets a little tricky," continued his father. "And that's the fun of it! But, after a while, you start listening to your intuition and figuring it all out."

"First you learn to distinguish positive games from negative ones," his mother advised. "I'll help you do that. Then you find you can choose which games you want to play. And finally you discover you have the power to raise above all the games - to understand what's really happening and to transform it all into harmony and fullness."

"Okay, I'm impressed! Such a splendid collection of games!" Adoni exclaimed. "May I choose any I wish?"

"Any and all the games you want. And there's many more we haven't mentioned," said his mother. "They all result from separation and amnesia."

But, again, Adoni felt a bit dizzy. "Speaking of amnesia," he struggled to ask, "why are you taking the trouble to tell me all this when, in a few moments, I'll forget it all?"

"Nothing of the kind!" said his father. "Remember, your Full Potential Self stays with us here in this Council of Masters on the Threshold. After you've planned your life from this vantage point, only your now - consciousness gets wiped clean as it tunnels into the third dimension."

"So, I really remain here on the Threshold?" asked Adoni, his mind still whirling.

"Sure, your Full Potential Self does! Didn't we say that?" puzzled his father, a bit concerned with Adoni's questions.

"Oh," interrupted his mother as she placed her soft multidimensional hand on Adoni's forehead. "You are definitely being affected by your proximity to the planet. You're already being pulled apart. We don't have a lot of time. Now that you've observed all these alternatives, let's plan your life - at least your first one. We're all here ready to help, and we each have our own parts to play."

Adoni Plans His Life

"Great! I've been waiting for this," expressed Adoni, as he suddenly regained his omniscience by focusing on this transcendent purpose.

So, with delight, which usually characterizes ascended masters, Adoni pulled out his completed questionnaire and announced his choices.

"At the beginning of my first life, I want to deprive myself of physical pleasures, deny my innate personality, disconnect from relationships, blindly conform to social systems, rationalize my basic principles and do whatever else is possible to totally sever my connection with the universal mind."

"Good! That's ambitious," observed his father.

"Then in the other half of my first life," continued Adoni, "I'll discover how truly miserable I am and find ways to transform most of these downdrafts into updrafts aligned with my Full Potential Self, in harmony with infinite knowledge, power and love. It'll be great fun!"

"Bravo!" exclaimed his mother.

119

"So much fun that I will probably allow a lot of the downdrafts of my first life to spill over into my second life, so I can come back and continue the fun as a woman." Adoni said. "I'm sure the second time I'll add to these games some clever feminine twists!"

"Oh you'll have a wonderful vacation!" approved his father. "So let's get busy planning that first life in detail. In about a 100 years, when you've finished that life, you'll come back here and we'll plan your second. Maybe then we can switch around the roles - maybe I'll be your son and you can be my mother."

"Is that allowed?" asked Adoni, not sure how far he could go.

"Sure, why not!" his mother said, as she smiled again and invited the entire group to gather at a round table in the Place of Planning on the Threshold.

The group then explored, diagrammed and delineated the games they would play together; and how they could help Adoni with all these experiences during his vacation on the Blue Planet, to bring about the fulfillment of both Adoni's desires and theirs.

Here Adoni made agreements with several of these masters to love and care for him even when he acts terrible to them. And others agreed to unconsciously love him so much they'd cause him great problems and pain, requiring him to look at what they really want, and to find the deep positive intent of their relationship.

They also planned when Adoni would have illnesses, accidents and traumatic experiences to jolt his memory and help him to reconnect with his Full Potential Self.

Finally, one of the masters, spending his last life on vacation, agreed to meet Adoni at the appropriate time and remind him of his real identity and what these games were all about. That would start Adoni's reawakening.

And what fun this group of masters shared, as they planned, laughed and joked anticipating all they'd experience together. But, of course, since they were still operating in hyperspace, this planning took no time at all.

When they were instantly finished, their Covenant was completed and Adoni felt prepared to go!

Adoni Organizes His Morphogenetic Field

"There's one last task to do before you descend," explained his mother.

"What's that?" asked Adoni.

"Your Full Potential Self must choose how to divide your total multidimensional personality into parts that support all these games."

"And how do I do that?"

"The mechanism is quite simple," noted his father. "You fashion a complete holograph of yourself and the universe and utilize it as the morphogenic field that manifests everything in your life. Of course, it's part of your total, infinite intelligence but it's specialized for use on your vacation."

"What do you mean?" asked Adoni.

"For one thing," said his mother, "it serves as the field that grows your brain and body on the Blue Planet, guided by your Full Potential Self here on this threshold. It will influence the sperm and egg encounter such that just the right DNA combinations are imprinted into the protein strings of your genes, which then influence your entire body growth."

"Then, as I said," continued his father, "it's actually the field that manifests your whole life. It's segmented into a thousand conflicting pieces, which support all these games you've chosen. Remember, we call these separate pieces your `holodynes - packages of thought that fill your conscious and unconscious mind on the Blue Planet."

"Certainly, 'holodynes!' It was mentioned in the brochure," recalled Adoni.

"These holodynes remain as resonating patterns in your subconscious, down at the quantum level of the microtubules of your neurons, where they set up resonating frequencies which cause your actions and manifest your games."

"How long do they do that? All my life?"

"Well, as long as you want them to," continued his father. "But whenever you wish, you can become conscious of any one of these holodynes, modify it back in line with your Full Potential Self and merge it again with your infinite intelligence."

"Great. What do I do now to set this up?" asked Adoni.

"Actually," explained his mother, "this will happen automatically as you tunnel through the third-dimensional barrier during your descent to the Blue Planet. All you do now is establish the mental morphogenic field, choose which polarities you want and decide which parts will be updraft and which downdraft, to coincide with your games."

"Okay. I now understand this part. But something still puzzles me." Adoni hesitated.

"Yes?" said both his mother and father in unison.

"Tell me again. When I'm down on the planet, amid all my games, pushed around by my holodynes, with so much of my knowledge, power and love hidden down in my subconscious, and most of that out of harmony with my Full Potential, what makes you think I'll want to discover and transform these parts of me? Maybe I'll just stay miserable all my life. Maybe I'll never make it back!"

"Don't fret!" reassured his father, realizing Adoni was becoming more dizzy by the moment. "It's no problem! That's why your lifetime is limited. When you die you automatically come back up here, enlighten your mind, transform your holodynes, merge with your Full Potential Self and prepare for your return to the Andromeda. Your vacation was a success! All your evil deeds and misery were just games anyway! And the negative effects you left on the planet will be transformed at the appropriate time during some other master's visit. It all balances out."

"But," noted his mother, "our experience with ascended masters is quite different. Most masters don't leave their vacation until everything is back in harmony. That's our cosmic nature, following the implicate order of the universe."

"Sure!" admitted Adoni. "I, myself, would feel a lot better leaving my vacation only after I've rediscovered and transformed myself and harmonized all the evil I created on the planet!"

"And, over time," his mother continued, "with so many ascended masters rediscovering and realigning themselves life after life, it progressively transforms this planet as a whole. If we keep this up, the place will become so advanced we'll finally have to select some other more primitive spot to experience our 'separation - vacation.' Of course, that won't happen for quite a while in 3-D time."

"Oh, good!" said Adoni.

"So don't worry!" his father concluded. "As you merge one part of you and then another, into alignment with your Full Potential Self, it feels fabulous, the most wonderful sensation you can have on that planet! The awareness of integrity! The sense of joy! The feeling of bliss! It's like coming home! When you taste it, you'll want it more and more. It leads you back to all knowledge, all power and all love. It's wonderful!"

For a moment, they stood, silently, gazing down into the Blue, feeling the oneness and wisdom of the universe they all shared. After a while Adoni spoke.

"I think I'll really enjoy myself up here with you masters watching the games our 3-D selves play together down there during vacation in our bodies."

"Yes," said his father. "It's the ultimate spectator sport! So let's get you on your way. We'll help you with this last step."

Thus, Adoni, the multidimensional ascended master, with assistance from fellow masters on the Threshold, made a holographic model of himself and the whole universe—his morphogenic field. Then he chose how to break it up into "holodynes," deciding where the third dimension would hide the pieces in his subconscious, way down in the water of his micro-tubules, making the eventual rediscovery of each piece very rewarding.

When Adoni finished, the morphogenic field was set, and Adoni was smiling a very large grin. "This is really going to be fun!" he said. "Humpty Dumpty putting himself together again!"

"Good!" observed his mother. "You look like you're ready to go. So step back into your transport vehicle and push the 'start' button. I'll give birth to you - in about nine months!"

Adoni Descends

Adoni took a few moments, shaking hands and waving goodbye to each master in this Place of Planning above the Blue Planet. All his future friends and enemies who loved him so much beyond time and space stood by as he reentered his transport vehicle and allowed his Full Potential Self to take over.

The 'start' button glowed red. With great anticipation he reached down and gently pushed it.

Instantly the quantum frequencies of the transport vehicle began to rise. These grew higher and higher until his whole being was prepared to support the vacation he had chosen. Adoni felt wonderful.

Then Adoni sensed the vehicle moving again. He was being pulled by the gravity of the planet into its field, slowly at first, then with ever-increasing velocity.

In a few moments, Adoni was plummeting toward the three-dimensional barrier at break - neck speed. "Wow, this is going to be quite a collision," he thought.

Just as this thought passed, the vehicle smashed into the barrier.

The impact was tremendous. A shock wave reverberated across Adoni's entire being. Abruptly, his Full Potential Self separated from his now - consciousness and seemed to step aside remaining on the threshold, watching the rest of the show from hyperspace.

Simultaneously, the mental holograph of Adoni, with all its knowledge, power and love, cracked into a thousand separate packages of energy - his holodynes. Some of the packages were positively charged and some were negatively charged, each according to the plan Adoni had just finished. Instantly, these were deeply concealed by the third dimension into his subconscious. At the same time, the impact wiped his now - consciousness completely clean, with no direct connection to his subconscious.

Thus, Adoni suffered amnesia.

Next, the transport vehicle, still carrying both his now - consciousness and subconscious filled with fractured holodynes, was abruptly sucked into one of the tunnels. There arose a high pitched buzzing sound and streaks of light rushed behind as the vehicle plunged down the dark passageway toward the planet at an ever increasing speed.

Suddenly, Adoni's now - consciousness was startled to find himself alone in a strange new place. It was warm, quiet and totally dark, surrounded by the sound of soft rhythmic beating.

Then he did something he had not done in a long time - at least for an eternity.

Adoni went to sleep.

Chapter Three

Sleeping Adoni Meets a Master

Thomas: "The same dynamics that created the galaxies created the stars and the oceans. The powers that build the universe are ultimately mysterious, issuing fourth from and operating out of mystery. They are the most awesome and numinous reality in the universe. Humans are these dynamics, brought into self-awareness, becoming now fully aware of our creative work. We already have these powers in the forms of stars, mountains, atoms, and elephants, but we do not have them in human form. We are probing still, exploring, experimenting. Having only just arrived on this planet, we are still learning what it means to become fully human."

Brian Swimme, *The Universe is a Green Dragon: A Cosmic Creation Story.*

"Throughout history, Dan, there have been blessed exceptions to the prisoners in the Cave. There were those who became tired of the shadow play, who began to doubt it, who were no longer fulfilled by shadows no matter how high they leaped. They became seekers of light. A fortunate few found a guide who prepared them and who took them beyond all illusion into the sunlight."

Dan Millman, *The Way of the Peaceful Warrior*

We can not teach people anything; we can only help them discover it within themselves.

Galileo Galilei

Well, as you probably expected, Adoni ended up asleep inside his mother's womb on the Blue Planet.

Bursting with potential, his holodynes were ready to play, Adoni was watched over by his Full Potential Self and, in about nine months, he was born in a body, with black hair and brown eyes, two ears, one nose and a mouth - like most beings of his species on that planet.

And there he was deprived of any visible power, void of conscious knowledge, and without his deep awareness of all love.

Of course, his parents loved him as well as they could. But, as they had agreed in the Place of Planning, their love was masked by the games they played. They named him "Donald," or "Don" for short, and imposed on him the belief systems of their family and culture, as all parents do.

Don grew up, studied law and business economics and became a member of a prestigious law firm in his home city. He also got married and had two children.

We now find him one summer, on vacation from his usual work, at a sunny beach on what is called the 'Black Sea.' The water is actually blue. The sand is white.

Don has brought some reading material, a book and a legal brief he never got time to study before he left home. He's making notes on his next legal case as he reads through the brief.

But the sun is warm. The waves' soft rhythm becomes hypnotic. He feels himself going to sleep.

Don Meets Vern, the Ascended Master Beach Bum

Suddenly, Don is aware of someone standing next to him on the beach, staring at him. Abruptly he opens his eyes and turns to see who it is.

The person looks like a beach bum. But there's a remarkable sparkle in his eyes. Something tells Don this is no ordinary beach bum. Just as abruptly, the bum addresses Don.

"Good afternoon. They told me I would find you here," said the bum.

"Who are you?" asked Don.

"Me? Well, I'm an ascended master, on vacation," the bum replied.

"A what?" Don asked in disbelief.

"An ascended master! On vacation! But even though I'm on vacation, I've been sent here on assignment to give you the secret of the universe, the key to dealing with the universe, and to tell you who you really are." The bum gave Don a knowing smile.

"What? Are you crazy?" Don asked.

"Not any more than you are," the bum replied, "I was sent here to wake you."

"Gee thanks," Don responded. "Please go away. I'd like to sleep!"

"I bet you would;" said the bum, "most people on earth do. It's part of their vacation. So how do you like yours so far?"

"What? My vacation? I like it pretty well. Nice weather! Good companions. Great!—except when somebody tries to wake me while I'm sleeping!" Don asserted.

The bum continued, "Excuse me, but everybody gets awakened in one way or another, sooner or later. We agreed to that before we came on vacation. Beside, I've been standing here for some time while you slept. I've been waiting patiently for you. It's only this moment that you noticed me."

Now Don starts to get intrigued by this very weird person. He decides to joke with him. "So you stood here and let me sleep did you?"

"Yes," replied the bum, "for quite a while. You're obviously enjoying your vacation?"

Don paused and looked at the bum, "Yes. Reasonably well. What did you say your name is, again?"

"My name is Vern," the bum smiled

"That's an interesting name. And what do you do?" Don asked.

Vern answered, "Lot's of things. Sometimes I'm an ascended master!"

"Sure! I'm sorry Vern," Don returned the smile. "You don't look anything like any ascended master. And if you were, I'm certain you'd take your position more seriously!"

"Oh really." Vern laughed, "They told me you are a lawyer, but you certainly don't look like one to me, in shorts and sunglasses laying out here on this beach, asleep. Why don't you take your position more seriously!"

"Well, I'm on vacation," Don asserted.

"Well, I'm on vacation too!" Vern replied, " Besides, whoever takes seriously being an ascended master, isn't really an ascended master!"

"Oh, I see," said Don.

Vern Teaches Don a Secret and a Key

Vern asked, "So, have you learned the Secret of the Universe?"

"The what?" Don pondered the question.

"The Secret of the Universe!" Vern restated.

"No," Don said, "I guess not. Sorry!"

"Well that's the first thing I came to teach you." Vern said quietly.

"Okay. So what's the secret?" Don was intrigued.

Vern paused, "Wait! You're not prepared."

"What do you mean?" Don asked.

"Look," Vern continued. "If someone was about to tell me the `Secret of the Universe,' maybe I'd want to prepare myself, like write it down, or something!"

"Oh, of course! Excuse me." Willing to indulge his visitor, Don gets out his pen and turns over his legal brief, ready to write on the back. Now, pen poised he looks up. "So, Vern, what's the secret of the universe?"

The beach bum kneels down and slowly writes with his finger in the sand. 'The Secret of the Universe: The Universe is already within you.'

"Come on," said Don, as he dutifully writes these words down on the back of his brief. "What does that mean: 'already within you?'"

Vern stated, "It means just what it says."

"How," Don asked, "could the universe be within me?"

"Easy - in your mind!" Vern waited for Don's reply.

"In my mind?" muses Don. Then in a quiet flash of insight: "Maybe that does make sense."

"Of course it does," said his visitor matter-of-factly.

"So I have the universe in my mind." Don thought for a moment. "Well, I never actually thought about it but that's where I keep all my knowledge about the universe!"

"Sure," Vern assured him, "and not just your knowledge but your feelings and your intuition and everything else! Now that you understand this, are you ready for the next part - The Key to Dealing with the Universe!"

"What?" Don was confused.

"The next part of my message." Vern said patiently, "I can't spend all day with you here, you know. I want to get some sun myself and some sleep too!"

In the moment, Don decided to explore the potential of this dialogue "Okay, okay! So, what's this Key!"

"Well," Vern explained, "knowing that the universe is already within you, I bet you can guess what might be the 'Key to Dealing with the Universe.'"

Don again pondered, "I never thought about that before."

"Well, if you want, you can start now," suggests Vern.

"Okay, so what is it?" Don asked curiously.

"You mean you expect me to just tell you again!" Vern paused.

"Wait! Aren't you the messenger!" asked Don.

"Sure," Vern replied. "But do I have to do all the thinking here?"

"No." Don answered, "I consider myself rather smart too."

"Good!" Vern exclaimed. "So if the universe is already within you, what might be the 'Key to Dealing with the Universe?'"

"Maybe," thought Don, "to deal myself, with that universe already deep within me!"

"Excellent!" Vern again exclaimed, "They told me you'd catch on fast!"

So Don writes, "The Key to dealing with the universe: Deal first with the universe within me." Then he suddenly stops.

"But exactly how do I deal with this universe within me?" he asks. "What do I do?"

"How do you deal with the universe outside of you?" Vern coaches.

"Well," Don replied, "I observe it. I interact with it. I find out how it works."

"And then what do you do?" asked the beach bum.

"Then I deal with it?" Don answered, unsure of his response.

"To get what?" Vern probed.

"To get what I want, I guess!" postulates Don.

"And to get what you really want, you help others in the universe to get what?" asks Vern.

"What?" Don was bewildered by Vern's query.

Vern explained, "All your clients, your friends, your family, the whole universe. What do you help them get?"

"Well," Don said, "I try to help them get what they want, I guess. And when I do, they help me get what I want too!"

"Certainly. Anyone who deals successfully with the universe learns this!" agrees Vern. "You got it!"

"Okay. But you're losing me a little. How does that apply to this universe within me that you mentioned?" Actually Don's wondering why he started dealing with this crazy beach bum in the first place. But their game goes on.

"Reflect on this a while." Vern paused for a moment, smiled, then continued. "You'll figure it out!"

"Fine messenger you turned out to be!" Don said half jokingly.

"Hey, sometimes a message comes in the form of a riddle. Solve the riddle, you get the message." The bum mused, "If I told you everything at once, you wouldn't appreciate it."

That answer catches Don. "I suspect that's true," he admits.

Vern Tells Don Who He Is!

"Maybe we'll get back to this in a few minutes. In the mean time, let's go to the last part. Are you ready to know who you really are?" Vern asked of Don.

"What do you mean - who I am!" suddenly Don feels offended. "I'm a lawyer. I handle important cases. I make good money. I've got a wife, two kids, a dog and a cat! I'm respected for who I am in the courts and in the community. I don't need any beach bum telling me who I am!"

"Fine!" Vern turned as he responded, "Okay. So I'll see you later. Bye!"

And with that, Vern starts off down the beach.

Suddenly Don felt embarrassed for being so abrupt.

He called out, "Wait! Vern! Excuse me! I didn't mean to be rude."

"Oh really?" Answered Vern almost 20 meters away.

"It's just that I get offended when somebody I don't even know tries to tell me who I am," Don explained. "Especially somebody who looks like a beach bum."

"You mean," Vern asserted, "someone who's on vacation like you."

"Yeah," Don half heartedly agreed, "I guess I look beach bummy too, don't I."
"It's okay." Vern said again with that knowing smile, "I understand. But maybe getting mad at people who try to help you uncover who you really are is a pattern you could look at more closely. It probably chases a lot of good information away. Besides, how do you know I don't know you?"

"Well, Vern, we haven't been introduced, have we? You aren't one of my clients. I haven't seen you at any of the social functions I've attended lately?"

Vern said simply, "No."

"So," asked Don, "how do you know me?"

"Well," Vern asked, "when you saw me, was there anything that looked familiar?"

"Familiar," puzzles Don. "To be honest, there is something in your eyes that caught my attention. I'm not sure I'd call that 'familiar.' But…"

Vern interrupted, "Maybe we're old friends, suffering from amnesia and we are just beginning to recognize each other!"

"Oh, yeah." This is starting to sound weird again. But Don was still having fun. So he continued." Okay, since we might be old friends; who am I, really?"

"Well," Vern said compassionately, "you're just like me and just like everyone else on this beautiful blue planet. We're all ascended masters on vacation."

"I'm an ascended master - too?" Don asked

"On vacation," Vern asserted.

Don replied with amusement, "Oh, right!"

"I know you don't remember anything." Vern continued to explain, "It's part of the game we play here. Amnesia! Hide and seek!"

Don really wanted to know, so he asked Vern, "What are you talking about! Why were you sent to tell me this?"

"As I said Don, everyone gets reminders now and then. They sent someone to remind me. And I started remembering. I'm getting over the amnesia we all suffer here. Of course, that's part of my game too."

Don asked Vern again, "So I'm an ascended master on vacation?"

"Yes." Vern reasserted, "Suffering from amnesia!" Vern turned to leave again. "Now that I've told you, I've performed my mission. So I can go back to my games on the beach! Good-bye!"

Vern Teaches Don to Access His Full Potential Self

"Vern, Wait. Is that all?"

"Yes Don. Unless you want more!" Vern turned to leave.

"Well. What else is there?" Don inquiry was sincere.

"Oh, everything!" Vern turned back and began to explain. "You can bring it all back - the whole universe into consciousness, if you want. All knowledge, all power, all love! However, you have to exercise unconditional acceptance. You must be open, perceive deeply, sense, with all your faculties, who you really are and what you really want. Then you learn how to ask for what you really want, from both the inner and outer universe, in a way you can get it!"

Don stated, "You're losing me again!"

"Okay." Vern paused for a moment, "Maybe I'm going a little too fast. Let's take it one step at a time. So what do you really want?"

"What?" Don asked. Vern continued his probe, "What would you really like to do, or to have, or to be, or to know?"

"Well," Don took a moment to reflect. "To start with, I truly would like to know who I am—really!"

"Okay, that's easy." Vern smiled warmly.

"Oh! I don't think so!" Don was flustered. "And in fact, I know a lot of other people who also don't think so."

"Maybe that's because they're just 'thinking.'" Vern knew Don needed further clarification so he continued explaining, "They're using the logical part of their mind that doesn't already know. It tries to analyze or extrapolate to answer your questions. But there's another part of you, your intuition. It already knows the answers!"

"Really?" puzzles Don.

"Yes," Vern continued, "But it answers your questions by feelings, imaginative pictures, visions and symbols in a metaphorical, almost mythical way, which the logical mind has difficulty accepting. And, most of the time, these answers are too subtle and too deep in your subconscious to be noticed - unless you, maybe just as an experiment, are willing to try some intuitive processes to get the answer."

"Okay. So how do I ask, intuitively?" requested Don, now quite ready to play along.

"Like this," said Vern, as he took a deep breath and patiently began. "First, may I invite you to simply relax?"

"Okay!" Don agreed. Vern waited a few moments as Don adjusted his position on the sand. He stretched his legs, drew his hands out from behind his head, letting them rest on his chest, and his eyes became fixed upward.

"What do you see? What do you hear? What do you feel?" asked Vern.

"I'm on the beach. I see blue sky above me. I hear the surf. The wind is blowing softly on my face," Don almost whispered.

Vern continued slowly. His words began to move in harmony with the waves on the beach. "Now just imagine yourself here in this beautiful place of peace. Envision yourself, enjoying the sun on your face, the wind in your hair, the sound of the surf against the shore. How are you feeling?"

"Quite, peaceful." Don was almost surprised.

"Good." Vern continued, "Now in your imagination, continue to enjoy seeing yourself on this beach. And as you do, look out a ways. Allow yourself to see coming toward you, a being - maybe person, maybe something else. And as you do, notice that it's YOU. And more, it's you the way you are meant to be, without any limitations. Your Full Potential Self!"

So, just as an experiment, Don let his imagination run free. As he pictured himself on the sand, he looked out, down the beach toward the horizon. In a moment he imagined his own figure walking slowly toward him. Then he allowed himself to be all he's meant to be! Somehow this figure took on a warm luminescence, a light from within. At once this scene seemed a bit unusual, but somehow, also quite familiar.

After a few minutes of silence, Vern suggested, "While you remain in this state imagining yourself, go ahead and pick up your pen. Describe what's happening."

Don half opened his eyes and lifted his legal brief. He started writing: "My Full Potential Self is me, all brilliant, radiant, powerful, and yet at peace..."

And as Don wrote, he continued to imagine his Full Potential Self approaching. He now felt a kind of closeness and warmth. He also sensed some qualities of his Full Potential: wisdom, patience, caring, and other qualities he couldn't quiet describe.

As Don now imagined this image approaching very close, he suddenly perceive a message. Though no words are spoken, Don distinctly perceives the phrase: "You are loved!" At the same time, Don experienced a wonderful sense of well-being.

"How do you feel?" asked Vern.

"Very peaceful. I sense wholeness and harmony." Don settled into this wonderful feeling within him.

"Good," says Vern.

Don slowly talks, his eyes still closed, focused on this inner world. "So this is who I really am - my Full Potential Self?"

"As much of yourself as you'll now allow yourself to comprehend." Vern smiled.

Don smiled at this answer. "That's an interesting statement. So now what do I do to allow more?"

Vern was happy to respond, "Start by getting to know this part of you. Spend time each morning and evening. Imagine going to this place of peace and invite your Full Potential Self to appear. Have a conversation. Receive messages. As you do this and similar processes, more and more will be revealed."

"Well," Don contemplated, "how interesting. It feels like a very effective meditation, maybe a good way of relieving stress?"

Vern took their conversation a step further, "More than that, my friend. It will open the door to your next level of fulfillment. Remember the riddle? Well this is one answer. It's a powerful way to deal with your inner universe, and get what you really want. But we'll talk about that at the seminar."

Vern Invites Don to the Seminar

"At the... what did you say?" Though Don's eyes were still closed, he raises his eyebrows with a puzzled look.

"Oh, I almost forgot to tell you," said Vern. "I teach these processes and a lot more in a training called 'Holodynamics' every month or so. The next seminar is coming up this Friday here at the hotel where you're staying. If you have some more interest, may I invite you to attend?"

"Sure. I mean, maybe. Let's see." Don was almost unsure how to respond, his eyes still closed, his focus still turned half inward.

"Well, that's it for now. Since I've done my part, I, too, want to get some sun and sleep. I'll be seeing you." And with that, Vern, the beach bum, disappeared down the shoreline. Don remained relaxed in the sun.

Don Awakes

Slowly, the sound of the surf again came to Don's ears. He opened his eyes and found himself alone on the beach. The images of his meeting with the beach bum ascended master still rested in his consciousness.

"Was this all a dream?" he asks himself. "You know, sometimes, the sun can get to me." Don began to collect his belongings and prepared to leave.

But then, as he picked up his legal briefs, he's startled. There, in his own handwriting, were the messages:

The Secret of the Universe: The universe is already within me!

The Key to Dealing with the Universe: First deal with the universe within me!

My Full Potential Self is me, all brilliant, radiant, powerful, and yet at peace.

I am loved.

"Well," pondered Don, "I guess some curious things can happen to you while you're on vacation."

Chapter Four

THE AWAKENING

With the active intervention of the intellect, a new phase of unconscious process begins: the conscious mind must now come to terms with the figure of the unknown woman ("anima"), the unknown man ("the shadow"), the wise old man ("the wisdom of life"), and the symbols of the Self.

Carl Jung, *Individual Dream Symbolism in Relation to Alchemy*

Still there are moments when one feels free from one's own identification with human limitations and inadequacies. At such moments, one imagines that one stands on some spot of a small planet, gazing in amazement at the cold yet profoundly moving beauty of the eternal, the unfathomable: life and death flow into one, and there is neither evolution nor destiny; only being.

Albert Einstein

The true delight is in the finding out rather than in the knowing.

Isaac Asimov

You remember we left Don the attorney and the vacationing Adoni on the sunny beach staring at the backside of his legal brief where he had scribbled something during his conversation with Vern, another ascended master on vacation sent to give Don a message. This is what he had written:

The Secret of the Universe: The universe is already within me.

The Key to Dealing with the Universe: First deal with the universe within me!

My Full Potential Self is me, all brilliant, radiant, powerful, and yet at peace.

I am loved and I am love.

"Well," pondered Don, "I guess some curious things can happen to you while you're on vacation."

With that, he got up and returned to the hotel where he was staying with his family. Don soon forgot about this incident with the beach bum. But later that night, while he was walking through the lobby of the hotel, he noticed a funny looking poster, which read:

Holodynamic Seminar – Phase I

Find Your Full Potential Self!

Don was very suspicious that this was the same seminar that Vern on the beach told him about. He checked with the clerk at the front desk, who verified that it was what he suspected. The seminar was set for the weekend, starting Friday night, and Don would still be at the hotel.

Something within him began to whisper softly: "Go to that Seminar. Go to that Seminar!"

At first he laughed it off and proceeded with his vacation. But he couldn't seem to escape the suggestion: "Go! Go!" So finally, he agreed to stop fighting himself. He decided to attend only the opening night, and see what this beach bum could possibly teach him.

Friday came. To his surprise Don actually enjoyed the seminar, especially the part that taught about the "Tracking" process, one of the "Ten Processes of Holodynamics" Vern outlined.

During the seminar and then over the next few months Don applied Tracking to many of the issues of his own life and those of his family and associates. He was amazed at the results. He discovered that many of the things he had been hiding within himself, once transformed, actually had the power and wisdom he had been searching for. He began to uncover a deep connection with his Full Potential Self. Don gained deeper knowledge, power and love. His life was more harmonious and successful.

Then something extraordinary happened.

One afternoon while he is driving home from work, his car hits a large hole in the road. The front wheel blew a tire. Don lost control of the steering. He slammed on the brakes as hard as he could but he was going too fast! The car careened over a metal guardrail and then crashed into a concrete pole squarely in front of the driver's seat!

In an instant, the collision jammed Don between the seat and the steering wheel with great force. The impact broke several of his ribs and severely compressed his heart and lungs. He could not breathe. The pain was blunted by a sudden numbness caused by the impact. Don appeared to lose consciousness and passed out.

Several days later, Don was regaining consciousness in the local hospital. The car accident almost killed him. His heart actually stopped beating in the emergency room shortly after he was brought in. The paramedics who transported him into the hospital had to work frantically to save him. But he was revived.

Now Don was resting comfortably in a hospital bed in a quiet part of the recovery ward. As his eyes opened, he looked up and smiled at the nurse who was finishing her work, gently wiping his forehead with a soft cloth. "That was remarkable," he whispered.

"Oh, you're back with us! You've regained consciousness," she said, returning his smile.

Then she asked: "Do you know what happened to you?"

Don stated simply, "Yes, I had a car accident, didn't I."

"You certainly did," the nurse responded.

"And a lot more." he quietly added. "I saw everything."

"Everything?" she asked. "You mean the accident?"

"Yes, and my whole life." he answered.

The nurse was curious. She cared for her patients and she knew that the first moments after they awake from a coma could be very important to their recovery. "Your whole life?" she asked.

"Yes." Don was weak but seemed to be gaining strength. "Let me tell you, because it's already beginning to fade."

"Okay," agrees the nurse.

"Well," he started very slowly, "there I was, suddenly floating above my wrecked car. It was very peculiar. I could see myself in the car, I could see that I was hurt, but it did not bother me. I was just inquisitive. There were people on the street that saw the accident. Wow! Were they astonished!"

Don tried to laugh but found his ribs were extremely sore. He adjusted his body a little and continued. "A couple of these onlookers came up to try to help me, but I was pinned in. One young man tried to open the door, but after several attempts he failed."

The nurse could now sense Don was reporting the accident as if it was happening again. But he wasn't concerned or worried. He appeared quite peaceful. He was a man who has returned from the dead.

"Next, the ambulance with paramedics arrived and freed me from the wreckage. They were so rough with my body I actually tried to stop them." Again, he let out a constrained laugh.

"Stop them?" the nurse asks.

"Yes. I tried to speak to them from my vantage point above the street. But you can imagine it soon became obvious that they couldn't hear me, so I stopped trying. One of them said 'Well this guy won't make it. He's gone already.' I guess it was then I realized I was going to die, but I didn't care. Everything was fine.

"Suddenly an interesting thing happened. Something like a tunnel appeared. It was round, dark, and surrounded me, pulling me into it. I no longer noticed what was going on at the accident scene. I found myself zooming up this tunnel with a whooshing sound in my ears.

There were things like lights streaking past me, and I sensed a bright light ahead. I felt great anticipation: I had to get to this light.

"When my trip ended, it took me a few moments to discover where I was. I found myself in a kind of garden. It was the most beautiful place I've ever seen. It was rich with green plants glowing with unearthly light. I looked at my own hands and realized that I too was composed of light.

"Then I realized I was not alone. People quietly began to approach me, and I started recognizing them.

"First was my father who died several years ago. He was dressed in white. He said nothing, but communicated to me a feeling of acceptance and love. I was being welcomed home. There was Uncle Ivan who died 20 years ago and Aunt Marina, his wife and many others. They appeared so radiant and so happy to see me! There flowed from each of them such amazing feelings with warmth and compassion! It was wonderful."

Don now paused a few moments to catch his breath. The nurse smiled. She had heard several stories like this from recovering patients who were near death. Each one was unique and yet beautifully similar. Still, she was worried about his condition. She asked: "Do you want to continue. Perhaps you should rest?"

"Oh please let me go on. This was not the most important part," he paused, caught his breath for a moment and then continued. "The most remarkable thing happened!" Don again paused. He was weak but his face showed how excited he was.

"A wonderful being of light appeared. This being was so bright and loving that I felt drawn to it immediately. It conveyed more love and caring than I have ever felt on earth and it engulfed me with its presence.

"That was overwhelming enough, but then it took me on a multi-dimensional review of my life. This was beyond words. Not only did I see everything I have ever done myself and with everyone else, but I could feel everything as well. I also knew how these events felt to all the other people involved. It was amazing!

"Understand there was no judgment offered by this being of light, only something like: 'This is your life. Are you satisfied with everything?'

"I felt great peace about my experience." Don was quiet for another moment. Then, just when the nurse thought he was finished, he began again. His voice was full of emotion.

139

"Yet I felt there was more. I sensed I still have something else to do here on earth before I die. It is not exactly a mission. I just have to accomplish some things to fulfill my life. I didn't want to die, at least not just yet." He paused again. "But I didn't want to leave the presence of that being of light, either."

Don went on urgently, "Please understand. I almost did not come back. This garden was the most beautiful spot I've ever known. I could understand so much all at once. So much, I comprehended; so much love! So much peace! I cannot begin to explain it. But somehow I felt I needed to return." Don managed another long deep breath.

The nurse asked, "What happened then?"

Don continued to tell the nurse about his experience "I felt the tunnel again. It was like I was being sucked back into my body. I sensed the hospital around me and I abruptly opened my eyes. There I was on this table with harsh lights in my face and a bunch of unfamiliar people bending over me."

"That was when they brought you in," she said.

Don explained what he remembered, "I guess the doctors had just finished reviving me, because, as I opened my eyes one of the attendants leaned over me and said, 'Well you made it!' His head was wet with sweat as though he'd been working hard. Surprisingly, that was the first time I felt pain. Then I suppose I passed out again. That's all I remember."

Don grew quiet and stared off into space. The nurse stood quietly by his side. Finally he added, "But I can never forget how peaceful that place felt and how wonderful was that being of light. It was so splendid!" Again, he paused. "You know, I believe I'm beginning to understand who that being is. Plus, I've learned some psychological processes I can use which take my understanding much deeper. Maybe I can get back to that place of peace. I may even be able to communicate again with that being of light. Yes. I'll give that a try."

The nurse waited a few more moments in silence. She sensed Don was finished now, so she insisted that he rest. Don went back to sleep. His body was very weak and required time to recuperate but his mind and soul were at peace. After a few weeks, Don recovered sufficiently to return home. He reentered his usual life, but this experience had a great effect on him.

Don no longer held any fear of death. He knew that he had more to do on earth and that he would do it. At the same time, he found himself enjoying the trip, without any anxiety. "What I'm to do next in my life is being revealed to me one step at time, as I continue to use the processes of Holodynamics," he said. "It's fun overcoming the amnesia!"

Within a few months Don began teaching Holodynamics at one of the Holodynamic Centers in a large city. The Myth of Adoni continues! In addition, each of us has our own myth to live.

Appendix B

The Code of Ethics

Principles of Personal and Community Discipline

Anyone in training or certified as a graduate by the International Academy of Holodynamics and who serves as an Advocate, Consultant, Facilitator, Presenter, Teacher, Master or Doctor and who is considered in good standing in this organization is an *Associate* of the Academy and bound by the following professional code of ethics:

1. RESPONSIBILITY TO STUDENTS

The International Academy of Holodynamics is dedicated to the education and potentialization of individuals, families, groups and complete organizational systems. As such, all those who profess to be an Associate of this organization are dedicated to improving the welfare of those who seek our assistance and will make every reasonable effort to ensure their conduct is always professional in nature, do all they can to guarantee individual rights and always act in ways appropriate for the integrity of the program. Therefore, let it be known to all that:

1.1 Associates do not discriminate against or refuse professional service to anyone based on sex, race, religion, group association or national origin.

1.2 Associates are cognizant of their potential influence upon students and do not exploit the trust of such persons. They do not use their position with this organization to create dual relationships that might impair their professional judgment or increase the risk of potential exploitation. Dual relationships include but are not limited to business, intimate personal sexual relationships or advisorships. Propriety requires that from six months to a year be allowed after training before any dual relationships materialize.

1.3 Associates do not use their professional relationship with students to further their own interests.

1.4 Associates respect the rights of students to make their own decisions and use educational processes to set up frameworks that help students understand the consequences of these decisions. All such decisions are the responsibility of the student.

1.5 Associates may continue a relationship with a student as long as it is beneficial to the student and will refer students to other associates or to an appropriate source of continued education whenever deemed necessary for the benefit of the student.

1.6 Associates do not abandon students without making reasonable arrangements for their continued education.

1.7 Associates obtain written consent from students before taping, recording or permitting third-party observation of their students.

2. PROFESSIONAL CONDUCT

Associates are dedicated to professional competence, integrity and conduct at all times.

2.1 Associates do not disclose personal or class confidences to anyone, except: (a) as mandated by law; (b) to prevent a clear and immediate danger to a person or persons; or (c) if there is a previously obtained, written waiver. In terms where more than one person is involved, all persons who are legally competent must agree to the waiver and then the information can only be disclosed according to the terms of the waiver.

2.2 Associates will only use student information in their writing; teaching or public presentations on condition that written permission has been granted, or when appropriate steps have been taken to protect the identity of the student(s).

2.3 Associates are subject to termination from this association and/or to other appropriate action when: they are convicted of felonies or misdemeanors that are related to their professional competence; have their licenses revoked because of professional impairment or mental incompetence; fail to cooperate with the Academy or come into open competition or opposition to the organization; or are impaired by alcohol or drug abuse.

2.4 Associates are dedicated to maintaining high standards of scholarship and presenting accurate information.

2.5 Associates seek to remain abreast of new developments in this and all related fields and to use this knowledge to teach others.

2.6 Associates do not engage in sexual, racial or any other types of harassment whether of students, trainees, employees, colleagues, research projects, companies, organizations or governments.

2.7 Associates do not attempt to diagnose, treat or advise on problems outside the recognized boundaries of their competence.

2.8 In all public and private conversations, Associates are careful to present themselves from a truthful, helpful and potentializing perspective, aware that their deportment has a powerful effect upon the lives of others.

3. RESPONSIBILITY TO THE ORGANIZATION

Associates respect the rights and responsibilities of other organizations and professional colleagues; carry out research, and participate in activities in an ethical manner, and help advance the goals of the organization in every reasonable way.

3.1 Associates remain accountable to the standards and ethics of the organization when acting as members, employees or representatives of the organization.

3.2 Associates assign publication credit to those who have contributed to a publication in proportion to their contribution and in accordance with customary professional publication practices and cite appropriately those persons to whom credit for original ideas is due.

3.3 Associates recognize a responsibility to participate in activities that contribute to the betterment of individuals, families, communities and society including donating a portion of their professional activity to services for which there is little or no financial return.

3.4 Associates obey the laws of the country in which they operate and are also concerned with developing laws and regulations pertaining to potentialization that serve the public interest and with altering such laws and regulations that are deemed not in the public interest.

3.5 Associates encourage public and private participation in the designing and delivery of services that further maturation and potentialization.

4. FINANCIAL ARRANGEMENTS

Associates make financial arrangements with students and third party payers that conform to accepted professional practices and that are reasonable, understandable and fair.

4.1 Associates do not accept or offer payment for referrals nor set up any type of kickback or pyramid payment schedules.

4.2 Associates disclose their fee structure before rendering services.

4.3 Associates do not charge excessively for their services and, when using materials produced by the organization, they do not duplicate such materials without prior written permission. When using patented processes, classroom procedures or techniques, Associates do not compete with the organization but pay and designated royalty and work in full cooperation with the organization.

4. Associates are careful to represent facts truthfully to students and other organizations regarding fees and services rendered and do not further individual profit or advantage at the expense of others or the organization.

5. ADVERTISING AND MARKETING

Associates engage in appropriate and truthful information exchange on both an individual and a public basis.

5.1 Associates accurately represent their competence, education, training and experience related to their teaching and the processes they use.

5.2 Associates insure that any advertisements, publications, phone listings, announcement cards, email, Internet, newspaper, radio or television presentations are formulated to convey accurate information. Associates insure that no claims are made that cannot be substantiated.

5.3 Associates do not use logos, trademarks, brochures or any patented information or processes that might mislead the public concerning the identity, ability, source and status of those practicing under the name of the Academy or the Association and do not responsibly hold themselves as being associated with an organization when they are not.

5.4 All professional identification used, all processes and course content presented, as well as all private or public presentations, business cards, office letterhead, brochures, advertisements or marketing materials of any kind, must be accurate, correlated and representative of the Academy or the Association in a responsible manner and cannot misrepresent services, qualifications or products.

5.5 Associates may use the logo, letterhead and any advertising or teaching materials of the association in any way officially approved through the head office prior to its use. All classes, as well as all special programs, research projects and ongoing classes, shall be correlated in writing with the Central Office of the Academy prior to their presentation.

APPENDIX C

PRESENTER PERSONAL PORFOLIO

This is your official record of your academic and field work as a Presenter. You must always keep your original in a safe place for your own records. A copy of this portfolio will be submitted to the International Academy of Holodynamics' Central Office and to your Sponsor prior to receiving your Certificate as a Presenter.

LOG OF PRESENTER ACTIVITIES

1. Courses Attended:

I have attended the following courses in Holodynamics since applying to become a Presenter.

Course	Location of Course	Presenter	Date	Sponsor Signature
Phase I				
Phase II				
Phase III				
Others (Name)				

My Name: _____

2. Activities:

Identify the Activity	Name the person(s)	Date	Time spent	Sponsor Signature

3. Other Activities:

_____

_____

_____

_____

_____

_____

_____

_____

_____

_____

_____

Activities refer to: field experiences directly related to Holodynamic Presenter training or duties such as participating in Holodynamic courses or meetings, using processes learned in Holodynamic courses to aid others and taking initiative on approved projects and leadership roles.

REFERRAL RECORD

As a Presenter, you may be awarded a referral credit for each person you recruit into any classes sponsored by the International Academy of Holodynamics. In order for you to obtain the credit, the person referred must declare on their Registration Intake Form that you referred them to the class. If more than one person was involved in the referral process, who gets referral credit must be worked out between the people doing the referring and reported to the Coordinator. Preferably, this is done without involving the person referred.

Referral credit may be collected as a *cash* reimbursement, if your account is paid in full, or it can be put on your account as *credit* toward Holodynamic classes you are taking or may wish to take in the future. In the true spirit of Holodynamics, this referral credit award is kept confidential. Credit is based upon a percent of the actual amount of money paid, and you, as a Presenter, must follow through to insure the greatest unfolding of potential for each person you refer. Here is a suggested format for keeping Track of referrals you have brought into the program.

Name of person referred	Address	Phone	Email	Date	Course

THE PRESENTER'S PLEDGE

I, (print your name) _____
herein pledge, on my honor, that I will take upon myself the responsibility to set my own prime conditions and join with a team that can help me accomplish this goal. I further pledge that I will maintain a "state of being" that sustains continued support for setting the prime conditions of others, particularly my own family and team members.

I pledge to extend my support to team projects and group activities. I pledge to support and set the prime conditions for the Holodynamic system and its missions that are aligned with my own Full Potential Self. Furthermore, I pledge to help facilitate the field-shifting processes and teach the advanced principles of Holodynamics according to the professional standards as outlined in the Code of Ethics and as presented within this manual. I pledge to maintain support in the setting of the prime conditions and the manifestation of the fullest potential of everyone and every project involved.

I commit to be present; to be alert to those possibilities that can add to the well being of the system; to team teach whenever possible, at the courses; to aid in the facilitation of small groups; and to follow through as Presenter in groups that may request or require my assistance.

I recognize the position of Presenter is a professional position of public and private trust and I pledge myself to a life dedicated to leading in the field to stimulate, in every way possible, the advancement of human consciousness. I acknowledge my team and this program as a living, conscious, Holodynamic reality and agree to take responsibility for my part in its creation and to help in every way possible to be present - to build a reality in which everyone and every part of reality can meet its fullest potential.

I pledge to support those who are aligned with these goals, regardless of race, color, creed, economic status, group affiliation or position. I acknowledge that pro-active projects will be launched toward the fulfilling of the fullest potential possible as a team and accept this as my course in life.

Signed: _____ Date: _____

Co-signed by Sponsor: _____ Date: _____
(as Witness)

A signed original copy must be presented to The International Academy of Holodynamics, 1155 West 4th Street, Suite 214, Reno, NV 89504. One copy must be retained by yourself and another copy must be retained by your Sponsor.

APPENDIX D

HOLODYNAMICS

THE NEWEST DISCOVERIES IN QUANTUM PHYSICS
For Unfolding the Full Potential in Your Life

THE NEWEST DISCOVERIES IN QUANTUM PHYSICS
FOR UNFOLDING THE FULL POTENTIAL IN YOUR LIFE

Life is Holodynamic.* That is, all life is part of one whole, dynamic information system. This view alters the very nature of what is possible in the human experience of life.

"Everything you have ever been taught is not true.
It is not that it's false, it's just that the truth is so much greater, so much more magnificent than anything you have ever been taught." Victor Vernon Woolf

WHY SHOULD I BE INTERESTED?

To transform a single holodyne is to change the "physics of your mind." All limiting thoughts and behaviors of your mind can literally be changed. This allows you to truly design your life and unfold your fullest potential. Once people understand the Holodynamic nature of life, they become "present" and gain the power to create extraordinary results in their lives.

In order to help people understand how to become present and unfold their greatest potential; we teach a series of seminars on "Unfolding Potential."

⇒ Learn the 10 processes of Holodynamics for achieving accelerated results
⇒ Transform holodynes that control your experiences, situation, beliefs and perception processes and access your personal power, wisdom and creative intelligence
⇒ Gain greater freedom of choice, strength and effectiveness in all areas of your life
⇒ Solve problems and are usually resistant to change
⇒ Develop more genuine intimacy
⇒ Become more effective on the job
⇒ Let go of unwanted habits
⇒ Maintain a state of being at peace, gain composure, master patience and organize your inner world to respond effectively even to turbulent times
⇒ Master the skill of unfolding the potential that drives every set of circumstances

---

* HOLODYNAMICS: nl. (ho-lo-di-nam-'iks), from "holo" meaning whole, and "dynamic" meaning effective force in motion. Holodynamics is the application of quantum physics, developmental psychology, information theory, holographics and other modern sciences to the understanding of consciousness and the unfolding of life potential.

** HOLODYNES: nl. (ho-lo-din's), meaning whole units of cause, refers to specific information systems that control thoughts, feelings, actions and consciousness of individuals.

WHAT OTHERS HAVE GAINED:

People who adopt a Holodynamic view -

⇒ Consistently solve complex problems in society
⇒ Develop open trust and faith in life
⇒ Become more prosperous and abundance-minded
⇒ Consciously maintain better health, overcome persistent diseases
⇒ Increase self awareness and dynamic personal growth
⇒ Overcome long - held emotional patterns
⇒ Reflect their new perspectives in their lives and communities

THE PROGRAM

Those who understand the Holodynamic view have organized a series of courses so everyone can learn this new and exciting view of life and gain, in an easy and fun way, the necessary skills to unfold their fullest potential. This process is sequential, that is, it is designed to move from the basics to the complex applications. Phase I, Unfolding Potential, and Phase II, Field Shifting, teach the basic principles and skills and are prerequisites for entering the next steps of the program. For those who seek further mastery of the skills, the academy provides an extended program of classes on *The Dance of Life*. These courses include five manuals and various levels of certification, and there is more.

WHO IS VICTOR VERNON WOOLF?

Dr. Woolf is Director of the International Academy of Holodynamics. Following his degrees in physics and education and religious education, as well as his Ph.D. in psychotherapy, he became active in transformative work with families, with drug abusers, the mentally ill, problem youths and prisoners. In 1984, he was asked to work in corporate America as a consultant and eventually began to focus on governmental transformation. He spent more than eight years helping Russia with their transformation from Communism and received many commendations for his contributions to science and society. He can, perhaps, be best described by the peace negotiations in the Middle East, where he is known among the Arabs as "Foraig," which means "solutions where none are evident." He is an outstanding motivational speaker and serves as personal consultant to individuals, families, and corporations where he helps create extraordinary results.

> *"Every problem is caused by its solution.*
> *Every challenge we face in life exists so we can manifest its solution." Dr. Woolf*

If you would like to spend some time with this amazing man or would like more information on how you personally can make more of a difference in the world, contact him by e-mail: academy@holodynamics.com or log on at www.holodynamics.com

Coming Up – Register NOW on line

PHASE I: UNFOLDING POTENTIAL

This weekend course teaches the first five basic principles and processes of Holodynamics including: Creating a Place of Peace, accessing your Full Potential Self, Tracking, (i.e. transforming your hidden information systems), organizing your mind via a Round Table and making the most of every situation by Potentializing. This is a transformational experience.

Once people understand the Holodynamic nature of reality, learn to track their immature holodynes and learn the relive/prelive processes so they can shift information fields, they have gained the power to create extraordinary results in their lives. In thousands of cases this has led to:

1. new understanding about health, disease and biological systems;
2. deeper self understanding, appreciation and self empowerment;
3. greater degrees of consciousness about consciousness;
4. greater degrees of freedom, more power to fulfill dreams and personal potential;
5. new levels of awareness about human development and growth;
6. solutions to individual and collective pathologies;
7. new insights and specific skills for developing intimate relationships and constructive, purposeful, mutually shared lives;
8. a more complete science of reality;
9. a better understanding of the relationship between human beings Nature and the universe;
10. a sense of greater connection with the wholeness of community and the living planet, how personal and collective intelligence functions, the mechanisms of collective consciousness and how to overcome collective pathologies and live beyond war, ignorance, hunger and abuse; and
11. integration of the information from the new sciences so as to be applied to the human situation, which sets the stage for the solution to most human problems.

For example, in this Holodynamic universe, according to the basic premises of quantum physics, every set of circumstances is driven by potential. Thus:

- every problem is caused by its solution;
- every person has a Full Potential Self; and
- every person can use their Full Potential Self to solve any problem.

For this reason, Holodynamics offers a series of seminars that teach specific skills on how to access the quantum potential field, give form to potential and manifest such potential in daily living. Participants learn to live life more fully and more consciously, which naturally leads to the solving of all types of problems and fulfilling every aspect of human potential. For example, in testing the practical application of Holodynamics over the past three decades, Holodynamists successfully:

1. overcame drug and substance abuse in six American cities;
2. reversed mental illness in 80 percent of the population of a state mental hospital;
3. rehabilitated hard-core criminals in a maximum security prison;
4. re-established academic standing for "at-risk" gang members in Los Angeles;
5. created a self-help program among juvenile offenders in Las Vegas;
6. established a coherence program for integration within large corporations in the US;
7. assisted in the successful "turnaround" of the former Soviet Union;
8. created a rehabilitation program among Arab terrorists in Palestine; and
9. created consistent positive change in the lives of hundreds of thousands of people.

Holodynamists provide a global educational program for individuals and groups. The program begins with an introductory course and progresses to advanced applications as follows:

Phase I is focused upon practical skills which insure increased consciousness for unfolding potential.

1. Internal Self-Management Processes
2. Integration skills and quantum coherence
3. the Holodynamic Mind Model
4. Potentializing in every set of circumstances
5. How to manage situational dynamics
6. Daily time management and master planning

Holodynamics Phase II - Field Shifting

This course teaches the principles and processes of accessing information that has been obtained from family and culture. This "information field" is held in common by groups of people and has great influence on every individual. Learn how to access this information field and transform it through a process of "reliving" and "preliving." Fields extend into multiple dimensions and parallel worlds of the past and future. Be prepared for a great adventure.

1. Life overview
2. The dance of the holodynes, human dynamics and games people play
3. Place of Planning, the lessons to be learned
4. The field in which the dance occurs
5. Family Genealogical Fields, their influence and potential
6. Field influences of parallel worlds
7. Field overview, family, cultural, transgenerational
8. Relive/prelive processes as part of field shifting

For your information, Holodynamists are currently working together to create the following:

1. a high quality, universally available computer-assisted education program
2. a global self-monitoring health diagnosis and treatment system

3. bringing to market new technologies that benefit humankind
4. actively involved in the social reconstruction of communities

People who adopt a Holodynamic view:

1. consciously maintain better health and overcome persistent diseases;
2. demonstrate increased self-awareness and dynamic personal growth;
3. become happier and more musical, active, involved people;
4. create deeper, more loving, meaningful relationships;
5. consistently solve complex problems in society and create new social orders that reflect their new perspectives;
6. develop principle-driven living habits, more open trust and faith in life and become more prosperous; and
7. maintain better ecological balance and a more universal perspective

Holodynamics - Phase III - Certification of Teachers

Holodynamists have requested the training and certification of 2,000 new teachers by the year 2010. In order to accomplish this goal, Phase III courses are being held (see SCHEDULE of Holodynamic Courses) to certify potential teachers. Certification requires applicants fulfill the academic and field experience standards of excellence as outlined in the Certification Manuals. A new text, *The Dance of Life* and five manuals, serve as the materials for certification (See BOOKS below).

The Certification Manuals contains:

1. Step-by-step principles and processes of teaching Phase I and Phase II;
2. Code of Ethics for all teachers of Holodynamics;
3. Required reading lists;
4. Role Play Situations with detailed instructions on how to use each situation;
5. Certification Procedures; and
6. Portfolio Management.

Business Courses

Perhaps the most electrifying breakthrough in the modern business world is the realization that there is no absolute reality out there waiting to be discovered. We all live, breath and have our being in an interactive, intelligent holographic universe that responds to our presence. Since reality seems to be dynamic and responsive, and since these sciences have proven to be the most accurate predictors available, their implications must be shared with the business world. This new information gives every business a distinct advantage. In order to share the leading edge, we have designed a full scenario of business courses that are created within specific business scenarios.

Intimacy Courses

One of the most rewarding courses for people take is the Intimacy series. The Academy offers classes on how to share your microscopic truths with others and how to hold a field that helps you manifest the fullest potential of your partner. We include practical experiences on how to cultivate the Being of Togetherness of your relationship, how to learn to work everything out, as well as communicate and celebrate life in a relationship that is alive, meaningful and coherent.

An Invitation

This is a personal invitation to you to sign up for the seven *Circles of Success* courses taught by the International Academy of Holodynamics. These courses allow local, national and international participants to have an in-depth experience of Holodynamics. Each course shows how to bring these principles into practical application, thus allowing both new and returning participants ongoing opportunities for potentializing themselves, their relationships and the ways in which they are manifesting every aspect of their lives. There are seven *Circles* and each has been created to maximize the potential that can be unfolded within a particular dimension of conscious development.

Every individual, every relationship and every system is managed by self-organizing information. Memory and other information are stored within the microtubules of every cell where it becomes self-organizing, alive and causal. Our holodynes exist within a quantum field dynamic that creates a morphogenic effect that resists change. In these classes, you will learn how to access holodynes and transform them in a specific area of consciousness. You are provided with powerful, yet simple tools for transforming your patterns and fully potentializing your inner world and your external world.

The Academy provides an arena in which we explore how our potential manifests from within the microtubules through holodynes. We have discovered ways to transform holodynes and shift the information fields of the past and the future. We have integrated these processes into the present and saw how our personal lives, relationships and social environments can be transformed and empowered. We have launched into projects for unfolding our fullest potential as individuals and as teams and unveiled some of the underlying principles that govern manifesting our own reality.

We explore the principles and basic assumptions that guide the emergence of life's potential, including the dynamics of principle-driven leadership as in the following:

- How to "hold a field" for the future
- How to set the prime conditions of individuals and of an entire culture
- How to "relive" the threads of collective consciousness from the past so as to align its potential with the present
- How to "prelive" the fields of collective consciousness from the future and set its prime

conditions through principle-driven leadership in the now

- How to manifest various aspects of the Covenant (our collective agreement to sustain a particular field of information), understand more of its dimensions and then apply these dimensions to the present
- How to move from collective deprivation to prosperity, from control to cooperation, from exploitation to coherence, from pathological co-creation to intentional communities, from slavery to self-sufficiency, from illness to health, from dictatorship to democracy, from pollution to production, and much more
- How to pre-invest the future, re-create our metaphors and rituals, and stand in the vortex of integration
- How to start in your own back yard, identify potential and team up to get what you want

You will learn processes for both field-shifting and field-building. You will receive instruction, be given practice time and receive an in-depth series of manuals for applying Holodynamics. Dr. Woolf's book *Holodynamics* reviews the principles and processes that have made a difference all over the world. His new book *The Dance of Life* provides the basis for the manuals. You will be given tools for accessing your field dynamics and you will be shown how to shift these fields through "relive" and "prelive" processes. Other holodynamists will be reporting on certain projects in which principle-driven leadership has proven successful. The field is ripe. The grain is golden. It is time to harvest. Let's go to work.

For more information, contact us at <u>www.holodynamics.com</u>

Or by e-mailing <u>academy@holodynamics.com</u>

Appendix D

REFERENCES

Beksey Von, G. *Sensory Inhibition,* Princeton University Press, Princeton.

Blue, R & Blue, W. (1996). *Correlational Opponent Processing: A Unifying Principle.* available at http://www.enticypress.com

Bohm, David. *Wholeness and the Implicate Order,* London, Routledge & Kagen, 1980

Bohm, David and F. David Peat. *Science, Order, and Creativity,* New York: Bantam Books, 1987.

Bracewell, R. N. *The Fourier Transform and its Application,* McGraw-Hill, New York

Brown, W. *Laws of Form,* 1964

Chalmers, D. *The Puzzle of Conscious Experience,* Scientific American, Dec. 1995

Chew, G. S. *The Analytic S-Matrix. A Basis for Nuclear Democracy,* Benjamin, New York

Daugman, F. G. *Uncertainty Relation for Resolution in Space, Spatial Frequency, and Orientation Optimized by Two Dimensional Visual Cortical Filters,* Journal of the Optical Society of America, 2(7), pp. 1160-1169, 1985

Freeman, W. *Correlation of Electrical Activity of Prepyriform Cortex and Behavior in a Cat,* Journal of Neurophysiology, 23, pp. 111-131.

Frohlech, H. *Long-range Coherence and Energy Storage in Biological Systems,* Journal of Quantum Chemistry, II, pp. 641-649, 1968

Gabor, D. *Theory of Communication,* Institute of Eclectically Engineers, 93, pp. 429-441, 1946

Ghahramani, Z. & Wolpert, D. (1997, March 27). *Modular Decomposition in Visumotor Learning.* Nature pp. 392-395.

Hameroff, S. R. *Information in Processing in Microtubules,* J. Theor. Biol. 98 549-61, 1982

Hameroff, S. R. and Penrose, Roger. *Conscious Events as Orchestrated Space-time Selections,* Journal of Consciousness Studies, 3, No. 1, 1996 pp. 36-53.

Hartmann, Thom. *The Last Hours of Ancient Sunlight,* Mythical Books, 1998

Hiesenburg, W. *Physics and Philosophy,* Allan and Unwin, 1959

Hempfling, Lee Kent. (1994, 1996). *The Neutronics Dynamic System.* Enticy Press.

Hempfling, Lee Kent. (1998). *The Rotating Turtle .* Enticy Press.

Kane, B. E. (1998, May 14). *A Silicon-Based Nuclear Spin Quantum Computer.* Nature vol. 393 pg.133

Kant, I. in **Wilber, Ken.** *The Eye of Spirit, An Integral Vision for a World Gone Slightly Mad,* Boston and London, Shambhala, 1997

Kohlberg, Lawrence. *Essays on Moral Development,* Vol. I, The Philosophy of Moral Development, San Francisco, Harper and Row, 1981

Marcelja, S. *Mathematical Description of the Response of Simple Cortical Cells,* Journal of the Optical Society of America, 70, pp. 1297-1300, 1980.

Penrose, Roger. *Shadows of the Mind,* Oxford University Press 1994

Piaget, J. *The Child's Conception of the World,* N.Y. Humanities 1951

Plato, in **Wilber, Ken.** *The Eye of Spirit, An Integral Vision for a World Gone Slightly Mad,* Boston and London, Shambhala, 1997

Pribram, Karl. *Brain and Perception: Holonomy and Structure in Figural Processing,* Lawrence Erlbaum Assoc., New Jersey 1991

Pribram, Karl. *http://www.bkstore.com/radford/fac/pribram.html,* Radford University Bookstore.

Pribram, Karl. *Quantum Information Processing and the Spiritual Nature of Mankind,* Frontier Perspectives, 6, (1), pp. 12-15, 1996

Rector, K., and Woolf, V. Vernon. *The Ten Processes of Holodynamics,* 1964

RICCI *the robot* at http://www.neutronicstechcorp.com/private/

Sheldrake, Rupert. *Lives of a Cell, 1988*

Spencer, Ronald G. (1997, November). *Exploring the Use of PNP Bipolar and MOSFET Transistors in Implementing the Neutronics Dynamic System* published by Enticy Press.

Scott, A., *Stairway to the Mind,* N.Y. Copernicus, 1995

Umbanhowar, Paul B.; Melo, Francisco and Swinney, Harry L. (1996, August 29). *Localized excitations in a vertically vibrated granular layer.* Nature pp793-796.

Vannucci, M. and Corradi, F. *Some findings on the covariance structure of wavelet coefficients: Theory and models in a Bayesian perspective.* Unpublished report. UKC/IMLS/97/05(1997, May).

Wheeler, J. A. *Assessment of Everett's "relative state" formulation of quantum theory,* Rev. Mod. Phys. 29, pp. 463-5, 1957

Wilber, Ken. *The Eye of Spirit, An Integral Vision for a World Gone Slightly Mad,* Boston and London, Shambhala, 1997

Whitehead, A. N. *Process and Reality,* New York, Macmillan, 1933

Circles of Success

This is the official **Presenter's Manual** for the fourth circle in the ***Circles of Success*** program sponsored by the International Academy of Holodynamics. This manual is part of a series and it is preceded by five texts: (1) *Holodynamics: How to Develop and Mange your Personal Power*, and (2) *The Dance of Life: Transform your world NOW! Resolve conflicts, create wellness and align your "Being" with Nature*, (3) *The Holodynamic State of Being: the Advocate's Manual I*, (4) *Presence in a Conscious Universe: the Consultants Manual II*, and (5) *Field Shifting: The Holodynamics of Integration: the Facilitator's Manual III*.

These texts and the ***Circles of Success*** courses are designed to help people apply the principles and processes of Holodynamics in their lives and to teach others to do the same. In order to assure the public that each graduate is professionally qualified, a **certification program** has been established. Graduates receive a certificate as they graduate from each *Circle* as follows:

Circle I: the Advocate: Anyone who advocates an inclusive view of reality qualifies at this level. The text for this level is an introduction to *the Holodynamic State of Being* which, once understood, is easy to support. Anyone can be an Advocate.

Circle II: the Consultant: This circle is for those who desire training in *Tracking* and other basic processes of potentialization. Once trained and certified, graduates can then professionally consult with others and are able to charge a fee for services.

Circle III: the Facilitator: The text for this level is *Field Shifting: the Holodynamics of Integration* and is focused on shifting collective information fields through, for example, the *relive* and *prelive* processes. Those who graduate as Facilitators can charge for their work with individuals and within small groups.

Circle IV: the Presenter: When you are ready to teach larger groups you can team up and teach the introductory courses on Holodynamic principles and processes. The text for the course is: *Leadership and Teambuilding: the Holodynamics of Building a New World.* Those who graduate are qualified to team-teach.

Circle V: the Teacher: This course is for those who want to teach without the assistance of others. Their text is *Principle-Driven Transformation: the Holodynamics of the Dance of Life.* Graduates are certified at the Bachelorate level by the Academy and are qualified to teach anywhere in the world.

Circle VI: the Masters Degree: At this level you will write a thesis and initiate a specific field project that makes a difference in the world. You will be certified to teach others to teach.

Circle VII: the Doctorate Degree: Those who successfully graduate at this level will have completed their academic training, written a dissertation and completed a major project in potentialization.

Those who successfully graduate from any *Circles of Success* course will receive a Certificate of Graduation from the Academy. Those who master the courses and complete their Master's training will receive a Master Certificate. The same is true of the Doctorate level.

If you are interested in taking the courses offered by the Academy, contact us at www.holodynamics.com or by email at vernonwoolf@holodynamics.com.